What people are saying about

A to Z of Mindfulness for Christians

David Harper's profound humanity shines through this precious book. It is both deeply rooted in his Christian faith yet open to wisdom wherever he finds it. It is a gentle book, with a knowledge of the complexity of the human heart. His own joy and peace, the fruit of years of commitment to mindfulness, shines through every page and is a foretaste of the fruit of the practice.
Timothy Radcliffe OP, Dominican (former Master of the Order) and Author (including *Alive in God*)

This book is a rare treasure-trove of insights from an author who has known both Christianity and Mindfulness from the inside. David Harper generously shares the fruits of years of deep practice and reflection, offering glimpses of what is possible when biblical wisdom is woven together with kindly awareness, nourishing the roots of faith and practice for all. The book has captured so well the essence of how mindfulness and Christian faith can nourish and sustain each other.
Mark Williams, Emeritus Professor of Clinical Psychology, University of Oxford, Co-author of *Mindfulness: Finding Peace in a Frantic World*

In a world of frenetic activity, mindfulness offers us an opportunity to pause and simply to be. This eminently readable and practical book is a Godsend for our fretful age.
Revd Martin Wellings, Superintendent Minister of the Barnet & Queensbury Circuit and author (including *M....*   *History*)

Dedicated to Sue, Tom and Sam, with thanks
for all your love and support.

Thank you to Sharon for proofreading and
to everyone at Circle Books.

A to Z of Mindfulness for Christians

A helpful, accessible, interesting book to help Christians explore Mindfulness and how it might complement/enhance your faith and spirituality

A to Z of Mindfulness for Christians

A helpful, accessible, interesting book to help Christians explore Mindfulness and how it might complement/enhance your faith and spirituality

David Harper

CIRCLE
BOOKS

Winchester, UK
Washington, USA

JOHN HUNT PUBLISHING

First published by Circle Books, 2023
Circle Books is an imprint of John Hunt Publishing Ltd., No. 3 East St., Alresford,
Hampshire SO24 9EE, UK
office@jhpbooks.com
www.johnhuntpublishing.com
www.circle-books.com

For distributor details and how to order please visit the 'Ordering' section on our website.

Text copyright: David Harper 2022

ISBN: 978 1 80341 116 3
978 1 80341 117 0 (ebook)
Library of Congress Control Number: 2022909177

A CIP catalogue record for this book is available from the British Library.

Design: Matthew Greenfield

UK: Printed and bound by CPI Group (UK) Ltd, Croydon, CR0 4YY
US: Printed and bound by Thomson Shore, 7300 West Joy Road, Dexter, MI 48130

We operate a distinctive and ethical publishing philosophy in
all areas of our business, from our global network of authors to
production and worldwide distribution.

Contents

Introduction

This book provides an introduction to mindfulness and how it is relevant and life enhancing to Christians.

I have found through personal experience, through much reading and listening, just how beneficial mindfulness is. By reference to a large number of passages in the New Testament, this book seeks to demonstrate how complementary Christianity and mindfulness are. I very much hope this very accessible book helps anyone with a Christian faith or interested in Christianity, to introduce how mindfulness might complement and enhance their faith, and, at the same time perhaps remove anxieties and objections

By exploring 52 themes relevant to mindfulness and Christianity, set out alphabetically, and drawing on relevant Bible passages, the book seeks to dispel fears and encourage exploration of how mindfulness might be helpful to you. Themes include words relevant to every Christian, including silence, time, compassion and worry. The reader can choose to dip into words which might be of relevance or concern to them, or, to read through from A to Z especially as Attitude is a good starting point and the topics covered under Y and Z are good places to finish the book.

Each theme can stand alone and could be read as a daily reading. Each theme has 2 quotations to contemplate and relevant Bible verses to reflect upon. The book assumes no prior knowledge about mindfulness.

Central to it all is Jesus – and in that chapter, each of the other themes is mentioned. Some frequently asked questions are addressed under Q for questions. The whole book seeks to address a whole lot more in a friendly and accessible style.

I very much hope you enjoy the book. Do visit the website and twitter page which relates to the book

www.atozmindfulness.co.uk

Follow me on twitter @AtoZmindfulness

Attitude

In your relationships with one another, have the same mindset as Christ Jesus.
Philippians 2 v 5

Whatever you do, work at it with all your heart, as working for the Lord.
Colossians 3 v 23

If you don't like something, change it. If you can't change it, change your attitude.
Maya Angelou

The longer I live, the more I realise the impact of attitude on life.
Charles Swindoll

The word attitude seems a very appropriate way to start this book. Your attitude will matter and colour the reading of the themes of the book which lie ahead. My hope is that you will have a positive attitude, an enquiring and open mind, to the themes that are being covered.

So, let us begin by considering this simple illustration about three people involved in a building project. Each of the three people is asked in turn, 'what are you doing?' The reply from the first person is, 'I'm carrying bricks – it's a really hard slog.' The reply from the second person is, 'I'm in the building trade, earning a decent living, and I'm grateful to have a job.' The reply from the third person, 'I am building a beautiful cathedral to the glory of God, and I am very privileged to have this opportunity.' Attitude to the task really matters!

Attitude makes a difference to not just our job, but to all tasks that we are involved with. An optimist thinks the glass is half full, a pessimist thinks that the glass is half empty, and, a realist knows that eventually someone is going to have to wash the glass. If the 'washer up' is you, then the attitude to washing up matters. Mindful washing up is a good learning activity.

Viktor Frankl (1905–1997) was a Jewish psychiatrist who spent 3 years living in unspeakable horror in a Nazi concentration camp. While he was imprisoned, he realised that he had just one freedom left: the power to determine his attitude to his appalling situation. So, Frankl chose to imagine, he chose to have faith, he chose to dream what the future might be like. And afterwards, he famously wrote, 'Everything can be taken from a person apart from one thing: the last of the human freedoms – to choose one's attitude in any given set of circumstances, to choose one's own way.'

Thomas Merton,* when commenting on the nature of contemplation and mindfulness, suggests that we should not look for a method or a system, but instead cultivate an attitude. He goes on to suggest that this attitude includes openness, attention, expectation, trust and joy and all of these can permeate our being with love. Some people refer to this as equanimity, a word that suggests impartiality to whatever arises, a relaxed and undisturbed ease.

The way to change your happiness level is therefore not to change your material well-being or circumstances, but instead to change your attitude towards your situation or circumstances.

This might eventually lead to a reappraisal of your aims in life or a new understanding of your spiritual direction. Things turn out best for the people who make the best of the way things turn out. A person's attitude to very small things also matters. I have found gratitude for very small things affects my day in a very positive way, and so I now tend to pray quickly and simply in a grateful and thankful way for small things. New Testament examples of Jesus doing this are found in John 11 v 41 (raising of

Lazarus) and Luke 22 v 17 (the last supper).

Sometimes a very simple task can be something to learn from. How we do that task, and, our attitude towards it, can tell us much. For example, I play table tennis in a room with six tables and a number of games happening concurrently. Inevitably, the ball will go off my table and under the feet of someone else's playing area. It is interesting how people respond to this. Some people just ignore the ball on the ground, some people kick it to one side, some people pick it up and pass it to the player on the next table. Some people even go as far as a smile or say thanks. For me, it is always good to pick up the ball look at the person I am passing it back to, and smile. This act makes a difference to my attitude, and it makes a difference for the other person, and in turn, affects their attitude.

Mindfulness is an attitude. It is an attitude that can permeate through all the activities of daily life. And it is an attitude that can have a positive impact on all aspects of day to day living. Paul encourages us to adopt an accepting attitude (2 Corinthians 12 v 9).

Possibility: at some point today, when faced with a task (which can be quite simple) that you anticipate you will not enjoy, take a moment or two beforehand to consider how it might be different with a changed, more positive attitude? Then do the task, and afterwards, notice if it was any different to your anticipation.

Awake

Peter and his companions were very sleepy, but when they became fully awake, they saw his glory and the two men standing with him.
Luke 9 v 32

And do this, understanding the present time: The hour has already come for you to wake up from your slumber, because our salvation is nearer now than when we first believed.
Romans 13 v 11

So then, let us not be like others, who are asleep, but let us be awake and sober.
1 Thessalonians 5 v 6

Those who are awake, live in a state of constant amazement.
Jack Kornfield

Today is life, the only life you are sure of. Make the most of today. Get interested in something. Shake yourself awake.
Dale Carnegie

The brilliant novel *The Book Thief* by Marcus Zusak, has a central character called Liesl, a German girl living in the poor outskirts of Munich, with her kind and loving adoptive parents. The book spans the time of the Nazi years in Germany. The family hide a Jew called Max in their basement. At one stage, there is great poignancy in the novel when Liesl is willing Max, who has lapsed into a deep coma-like sleep, to wake up, to live. There is great jubilation when Max does indeed wake up, when he takes these first steps to being awake and alive. Being awake has two stages: firstly, not being asleep and secondly, being alert to what is going on around you.

There are many instances in the New Testament when Jesus encourages those around him to stay awake. This is particularly the case with the disciples, who He teaches and encourages to become witnesses, leaders and evangelists of the embryonic Christian movement. Even at the scene of the transfiguration, Peter and the companions were overcome with sleep. When they became fully awake, they could see the glory of Jesus in the transfiguration. You might have expected that they would have been awake and alert to what Jesus wanted them to see. But Peter and the others are human, they show human traits of tiredness and lethargy. Jesus wanted the disciples to keep awake not just for themselves, but also for those around them. Similarly, keeping awake is not just for ourselves, but also for those around us.

CS Lewis wrote (in Letters to Malcolm), 'We may ignore, but we can nowhere evade, the presence of God. The world is crowded with him. He walks everywhere incognito. And the incognito is not always hard to penetrate. The real labour is to remember, to attend ... in fact to come awake. Still more, to remain awake.' Even during the times when we have our eyes open, it is still possible for us not to be awake. It is still possible for us to sleepwalk! I don't mean literally. I mean metaphorically: it is possible for us to sleepwalk through our whole lives.

The teachers of mindfulness call this condition of not being awake being on autopilot. What is meant by this phrase of being on autopilot? Examples of when you are on autopilot might include the following: travelling to work, going on the 'school run', going to the supermarket. Being on autopilot means carrying out activities without giving them any attention at all. Being on autopilot means not being awake to sounds, sights or smells that are around. Being on autopilot means not giving those around us any attention. It is possible for us to do this day after day, week after week and if we are not careful, year after year. Being awake is being ourselves. Being awake is being present. Being awake is bigger than individual thoughts.

What might we do to help ourselves stay awake? To stay aware? One way we might help to stay awake is by focussing on the breath. We simply give attention to the breath as it is inhaled and exhaled, inspired and expired. The in-breath is 'inspiration', giving you energy and life, each and every time, alerting heart and mind and spirit. In the Genesis story, God breathes into the lungs of Adam. In the New Testament Jesus breathes into the disciples. The breath of Jesus flowed into the disciples. It was a gift from Jesus to the disciples. It connected them together. The love of Jesus was tangible, physical and real.

The Greek word for breath and spirit and wind all come from the same word *ruach*. There is a reciprocal link between the breath and the physical state. As we spend a few moments reconnecting with the breath, becoming awake to the breath, then we can become wholly awake.

The breath for us is tangible, physical and real. Breathing is evidence and a sign that we are alive. When a body is alive, breath happens and pulse happens.

Martin Luther King* eloquently put it like this: 'One of the great liabilities of history is that all too many people fail to remain awake through great periods of social change. Every society has its protectors of status quo and its fraternities of the indifferent who are notorious for sleeping through revolutions. Today, our very survival depends on our ability to stay awake, to adjust to new ideas, to remain vigilant and to face the challenge of change.' Mindfulness can help us to stay awake in all kinds of ways.

Possibility: in one situation today, seek to be really awake and alert – so that as you look and experience, you are not indifferent, resentful, judgemental but instead open and loving.

Body

The Word became flesh and made his dwelling among us.
John 1 v 14

May God himself, the God of peace, sanctify you through and through. May your whole spirit, soul and body be kept blameless at the coming of our Lord Jesus Christ.
1 Thessalonians 5 v 23

Health is a state of complete harmony of the body, mind and spirit.
BKS Iyengar

Take care of your body as if you were going to live forever; and take care of your soul as if you were going to die tomorrow.
Saint Augustine

One of the many difficult words for Christians to get to grips with is 'incarnation'. In simple terms, this means that God came to earth in human form, God came in a human body (John 1 v 14). Jesus says many profound things in the gospels. The power of what He said was made more powerful by His living body backing up His living words. Jesus embodied truth and faith. (He 'walked the talk'.) The Old Testament seems to be an attempt by God to express the connection to humans through words and rules (e.g., 10 commandments) but this connection doesn't fully succeed. God had to try another way (Luke 20 v 9–15) in the form of a body, the body of Jesus. And by doing this, through the physical body of Jesus, God connects completely to us.

Over the centuries, many Christians and theologians have sought to separate the mind and body (academics call this dualism), often with the suggestion that the mind is 'good' and the body 'not good', but Thomas Aquinas* suggested that 'we should love our bodies with the same charity with which we love God' quoted in Timothy Radcliffe* *Alive to God* p. 282. Timothy Radcliffe goes on to explain 'Christianity is a very physical religion ... so our bodily life – hearing, seeing, touching, walking, eating and drinking – is made holy in the Lord.' This means that we need to have more respect for, and make greater connections to, our bodies. Mindfulness involves an awareness of our body. In the Mindfulness A Practical Guide to Finding Peace in a Frantic World course,* one of the mindfulness practices is called the Body Scan. In this practice, the participant is invited to connect with each part of the body. The body scan is not easy! At times it can seem boring. Depending on attitude, then, at times it can seem even pointless.

I do believe that there is no such thing as disembodied mindfulness. Mindfulness is body, breath and mind (and the interaction between all three). For example, I notice that when I'm facing a situation which I am anxious about (e.g., an interview), I have butterflies in my tummy. Other people suffer from perspiration, others brightness around the neck or shortness of breath. The events in your body such as stomach rumbling, cold feet, an itchy head are all things that are happening in the present moment. Some of these events may be pleasant, some of these events may be unpleasant. A mindful attitude can help with these bodily reactions. As part of the Body Scan, participants are sometimes encouraged to breathe towards an area of pain or tension. Many say that the act of breathing towards the area of tension can make a difference. People who do yoga, Tai Chi or similar practices, become more connected to their bodies, to their breath, their balance, and also to sources of tension. A number of years ago, I tried yoga. But I always seemed to feel stiff and awkward, particularly as I compared myself with others despite the teacher repeatedly saying not to do this! (I hadn't come to mindfulness then!) Mindfulness helps

9

us redress this balance of detachment from our bodies. Instead of detachment we can welcome ourselves home to our bodies, connecting more fully with them.

Much has been written about body language, and how much it informs other people far more than the words we use. Perhaps, by becoming more aware of our bodies, we can inform ourselves at the same time as we inform others. What is going on in our mind shapes our body. For example, when we are defensive, anxious or depressed we fold in on ourselves – we slump, we cross our arms in front of us When we are happier, then our body shape opens up. When working at Oxford University I came across a very intelligent young female student, who was sectioned into the specialist unit of the Oxford hospital which deals with eating disorders. I could not begin to understand why it was that she wanted her body to be so slight and get her BMI so low that it became life-threatening. I found it so sad that her relationship with her body had reached this desperate state.

When the body suffers, so can the mind. When the mind suffers, so does the body. Our inner being and outer being are so interconnected. What happens on the outside (pain, aching, pleasurable sensations) can affect what happens on the inside. What happens on the inside (fear, anxiety, hope) can affect what happens to the body on the outside. Mindfulness can help. Mindfulness can help to relieve bodily pain. Jon Kabat Zinn* found this in his work in the United States. Ruby Wax* refers to this in her book *Sane New World*. So, if you are someone who spends much more time in your head, thinking and analysing – there is another option! Reconnecting to your body.

Possibility: if you have something to do today that makes you a little anxious, take a moment or two to notice where there might be tension in your body when you are about to start, and while you are doing the activity. Reflect on this.

Breath

And with that, He breathed on them and said, 'Receive the Holy Spirit.'
John 20 v 22

And He is not served by human hands, as if He needed anything. Rather, He himself gives everyone life and breath and everything else.
Acts 17 v 25

Then the Lord God formed a man from the dust of the ground and breathed into his nostrils the breath of life; and the man became a living being.
Genesis 2 v 7

Every moment allows you the opportunity to take a deep breath in and be grateful for the fact that you can take in a breath.
John Assaraf

Breathing in, I come to body and mind. Breathing out, I smile. Dwelling in the present moment, I know this is the only moment.
Thich Nhat Hanh

Stating the obvious, every person that is alive is breathing! It is something that we all do, every nationality, every culture group, every religious group, every political group, atheists, agnostics, Christians. And among the Christian community, conservatives, evangelicals or liberals, each one of us is breathing, each and every day, each and every moment. The coronavirus suddenly made things different for the whole world. Suddenly many thousands of people needed assistance with breathing, suddenly ventilators were required in huge numbers. This became a scary aspect of this terrible virus.

We can only breathe now. It is not possible to breathe for yesterday, or for an hour ago. We cannot breathe for when we recently had an argument with our partner or spouse. We are not able to breathe for tomorrow, when we might have a difficult meeting with our line manager, or when we are going on holiday. The only time that we can breathe is now. The only time is here. The only time is in this moment. And how we breathe, affects our body and our well-being. People notice that in certain situations, the speed of breathing changes involuntarily. During interviews, in situations of conflict, or when a public speech needs to be given, breathing for many people happens both faster and shallower. And this change in breathing has a negative impact on the amount of oxygen getting to the brain. To re-establish more oxygen, the technique is to deliberately breathe more slowly, and, breathe more deeply. Not only does this assist with increasing levels of oxygen, it also promotes a greater sense of calm.

Matthew Syed writes about the need for ten thousand hours of practice if you are to become the best at any particular sport. Syed refers to tennis, golf and chess champions, and all kinds of people who have reached the best in their chosen sport. We have many, many hours of breathing, but not so many hours of attentiveness to breathing. Rather than 10,000 which is huge, I believe that 100 hours or even 10 hours of real attention to our breathing might make a real and significant difference to the way that we breathe. Attentive awareness to the breath takes practice, lots of practice, but the practice is worth it and pays dividends.

We might consider breathing in and out as a sacred connection to God. In each and every moment, each in-breath and each out-breath, not just physical breath but also spiritual breath. Jesus breathed on his disciples, and by doing so, connected with the creation story when God breathes into the human race. In Genesis, the creative wind, or, breath of God, sweeps over creation. The breath is a gift given to us each and every moment, the gift of life is given to us each and every moment. The gift of the breath is not just for ourselves. The gift of the breath gives us life and energy and the ability to reach out and communicate with and connect to others. Many mystics and contemplatives discovered the breath as a connection to God, a way of narrowing or dispelling the separation from God. They learnt to breathe God in, breathe God out to all sentient beings.

Guided mindfulness meditations, whether as part of a group, or listening to a CD, phone app or via the Internet, is how we might actually practise giving more attention to the breath. In many guided mindfulness meditations, the breath is referred to as an anchor, something on which we can focus the attention, something that helps us take our attention from worrying and intrusive thoughts. The guided meditation will often direct participants to an awareness of the breath in various stages of inhalation and exhalation. One particular way that the meditation gets started is by focussing the attention on where the breath is most noticeable (which might be in the nose or the mouth, or might be much deeper in the body towards the abdomen). And later, most meditations will spend some time focussing on the abdomen expanding and contracting. Some people find it helpful to put their hand on the abdomen to increase the sensation of the inhalation on the exhalation. Then in many of the guided meditations, participants are working to maintain their focus on the breath in the abdomen in silence. This can be quite hard! This can be the time when the mind gets busy.

What I have found when guiding other people with these meditations, is to invite them to use a very simple mantra in the periods of silence if their minds have become busy. The simple mantra is said silently to oneself: 'just this breath in' and 'just this breath out'. Alternatively, counting each in-breath,

breath 1, breath 2,… up to breath 10. And repeating if necessary. Personally, I have found these two options very useful when my mind has been particularly busy. And then what I notice, is that the breath quietens and deepens. And as the breath quietens and deepens, we become more ourselves.

Possibility: for a short time, find a comfortable and alert sitting position. Draw attention to your breath. Each time you become distracted, return to the breath. If required, use any of the suggestions above.

Change

Do not conform to the pattern of this world, but be transformed by the renewing of your mind.
Romans 12 v 2

So you are no longer a slave, but God's child; and since you are God's child, God has made you also an heir.
Galatians 4 v 7

Nothing is so painful to the human mind as a great and sudden change.
Mary Shelley

Isn't it funny, how day by day nothing changes, but when you look back, everything is different?
CS Lewis

We are in a fast-changing world. And the speed of change is not linear, but exponential. For some, personal computers and laptops and tablets have always been around. Not so for all of us.

A computing option formed part of my management sciences degree at Warwick University. It involved taking punch cards to a computer room, leaving them overnight and waiting to receive a printout the next morning! It is very hard to believe now, that this was very advanced at the time. Computing has changed our lives dramatically, particularly thanks to Tim Berners Lee gifting the world the Internet. The immediate availability of information changes life radically. Smart phones, which are owned by huge numbers of the world population, including quite young children, have changed lives irrevocably (e.g., positively by giving poor farmers in Africa access to online banking, negatively by giving lonely people access to pornography). Because we are assimilating so much information, so much more quickly, we need strategies to help us cope. All kinds of changes have happened to every aspect of our lives. These include attitudes to race relations, gender fluidity, transport, family life, work, lifestyles in general. This is all highlighted by the different voting preferences of the old and the young (e.g., Brexit), which is informed by significant differences of attitude to many contemporary issues. Change is at an individual, community level and national/international level.

I really like the word *metanoia*. For me, it is a lovely word with positive associations. Maybe because it's a Greek (or non-English) word to which we can attach or attribute meaning. In contrast, the word repentance I find a more difficult word, with a long history of negative connotations. For Christians, *metanoia* is often thought of as a one-off experience (e.g., Paul on the road to Damascus). For me, at the age of eighteen, I attended a 'tent crusade' in Didcot, and 'went forward' to make a commitment – making a change: of heart and mind. This is the moment in my life which I view as when I turned to God and became a Christian. However, *metanoia* happens every single day and many times a day – choices and changes of heart and mind. A metaphor often used to describe progress in Christian discipleship is a journey. But the journey we are on is not simply getting on a train and travelling down a prescribed track. Rather, it is keeping awake, getting out at different stations, and being alert to which train to catch next. In this way the journey is varied, interesting and developmental.

Sometimes, however, the change of direction that we need to make is quite dramatic. A powerful illustration of this by Jesus is the tale of the prodigal son. The son makes one journey away from his father, from love and care. Then later, he has a *metanoia* change of direction, he comes to his senses, he turns around completely, and makes a journey back towards his father, and his father's love and care. In the story, the father is always present, waiting, hoping. It is the prodigal son who 'goes missing'. In our lives, God is always present, waiting, hoping. And it is us who sometimes 'go missing', drifting away into our own world, into our own ego driven activities. And it is possible that we can go missing for hours, for days or even longer. The younger son has a 'light bulb moment', and as a result he turns back. In the 'light bulb moment' for us, when it comes to our attention, we can make a *metanoia* change and turn back towards God. Mindfulness can lead to *metanoia* moments, by embracing or making a change towards new habits of being in the present moment, new habits of being, new habits of the mind. This kind of *metanoia*, this kind of change, is a positive one.

In the Mindfulness A Practical Guide to Finding Peace in a Frantic World course,* one of the chapters relates to 'facing the difficult'. Sometimes, the *metanoia* change we might need to make involves turning towards pain and difficulty rather than turning away from it. It can be an extremely hard part of the course and when participants are involved in this they need to be in good hands. I cannot emphasize enough how important it is to be in the hands of those who are fully trained and qualified. When exploring mindfulness further, please take care (and also go to the theme 'You and what next' if you would like to think about this a little more).

Possibility: make one simple change today, e.g., where you sit at lunch. Notice what effects this has? What do you see and notice?

Compassion

But a Samaritan, as he travelled, came where the man was; and when he saw him, he took pity on him. He went to him and bandaged his wounds, pouring on oil and wine. Then he put the man on his own donkey, brought him to an inn and took care of him.

Luke 10 v 33–34 (as part of v 30 to 37)

When he saw the crowds, he had compassion on them, because they were harassed and helpless, like sheep without a shepherd.

Matthew 9 v 36

Therefore, as God's chosen people, holy and dearly loved, clothe yourselves with compassion, kindness, humility, gentleness and patience.

Colossians 3 v 12

Compassion and tolerance are not a sign of weakness, but a sign of strength.

Dalai Lama

Our task must be to free ourselves, by widening our circle of compassion to embrace all living creatures and the whole of nature and its beauty.

Albert Einstein

One of the very best-known stories in the gospel is that of the Good Samaritan. The very phrase has entered into our language and describes in general terms the act of one person showing compassion to another person. Margaret Thatcher famously referred to this story by saying that a Good Samaritan was only able to provide assistance because he was rich. I do not think she was right – in that we are all able to carry out these acts of compassion, acts of kindness, acts of selflessness. And my observation is that these acts are often carried out by those who are not materially rich.

As He told the story, Jesus indicates that the Samaritan carries out his acts of compassion without expecting something in return. What the Samaritan did was not conditional. The person that he helped was actually unconscious and did not know who was helping him. The victim on the roadside had no idea that the compassion was coming from somebody who was different socially, culturally and ethnically. But despite all these differences, the Samaritan just gave compassion to this helpless stranger.

One lesson to be learned from the story of the Good Samaritan is that the compassion needs to be at the right time in the right place. The Good Samaritan acted there and then, in that very moment. Had he delayed, perhaps a day or two, put off the assistance that he gave, it may well have been too late and the victim may have died. Compassion was his natural response at that moment. And at the end of the passage, the encouragement from Jesus is for us to go and do likewise. It is not just an entertaining story. It is an encouragement towards a lifestyle, a lifestyle of compassion, a lifestyle where you love your neighbour as yourself. And as we become more compassionate, then we discover more of the compassion of God.

Compassion, then, is experiential. Compassion is not just thoughts, but also action. In the story, both the priest and the Levite have thoughts and actions. In both cases, they see a victim on the roadside and their thought is to not get involved, which leads to the action of crossing the road. In complete contrast, the Samaritan sees the victim, has the thought 'what can I do?', and based upon that thought carries out acts of compassion. Compassion can be tarnished or even corrupted by fear, by indifference, by the self-seeking ego. Some argue that it's difficult to have wisdom without compassion. It is interesting that the word compassion, the word patience, the word endurance, and the word suffering all come from the same Latin root word *patior*.

If God is compassionate to us then, surely, we can learn to be self-compassionate, because the command is to love our neighbours *as ourselves* (Mark 12 v 30–1). There is much evidence to show that those who are truly self-compassionate, are more able to show compassion to others. This makes sense to me. If we have come to a good and compassionate understanding of ourselves, we might then have a greater understanding and empathy for others. And if we can show compassion to the whole of ourselves, not just the church bits, not just the bits that other people praise, not just the bits that make us feel warm inside, but the whole of ourselves then this will provide much more of the abundant life (zest) Jesus wants us to have.

In the Mindfulness A Practical Guide to Finding Peace in a Frantic World course,* there is a guided meditation called the loving kindness guided meditation which is where you wish various people compassion (similar to and yet different from prayer). The part that I found hardest was compassion to self. Of course, being compassionate to the person brought to mind that you love wasn't too hard, but incredibly I found it was easier to be compassionate to the person brought to mind who was a stranger at the bus stop than it was to myself. Now, looking back, this is just incredible to notice and reflect upon. But it might also be the case for you. For me, even more vital than the self-compassion in the guided meditation, is the formation of a habit of self-compassion during every moment of the day. This can make a huge difference.

When you gain more understanding of yourself, compassion can become easier. Once you begin to understand the impact of your childhood, your schooling, your siblings and your parents, the very complex unique and loveable person that you are becomes easier to understand. I have recently started listening to the back catalogue of *Desert Island Discs*. It is clear from listening, that the early experiences (positive and negative) of the guests demonstrate the impact they have on their lives. I know this from my own experience as a child. By the age of 12, I had lived in 3 different countries, 8 houses, and attended 5 schools. These changes had an impact. I recognise that this has made me very sensitive to the views of others, and this sensitivity, coupled with a very conservative Christian outlook in my very early days of faith, has resulted in a life of little self-compassion. A good friend asked what if our current situation is not where we wish to be? Well, the current situation is where we are. And a self-compassionate attitude makes all the difference to being able to survive, or possibly even thrive in that situation. In all our circumstances, even when we are making mistakes, God still loves us.

Possibility: say the serenity prayer 'God, grant me the serenity to accept the things I cannot change; courage to change the things I can; and wisdom to know the difference'. And afterwards spend a few moments compassionately seeking to know the difference about one or two aspects of your life.

Divine (contemplation)

Then Jesus said, "Whoever has ears to hear, let them hear."
"Consider carefully what you hear," he continued.
Mark 4 v 9, 23

Thus, by their fruit you will recognize them.
Matthew 7 v 16

Very early in the morning, while it was still dark, Jesus got
up, left the house, and went off to a solitary place where he
prayed. Simon and his companions went to look for Him, and
when they found Him, they exclaimed 'Everyone is looking
for you.' Jesus replied, 'Let us go somewhere else, to the
nearby villages, so I can preach there also. That is why I have
come.'
Mark 1 v 35–39

What we planted in the soil of contemplation; we will reap in
the harvest of action.
Meister Eckhart

God comes to us, disguised as our life.
Richard Rohr

For my last four working years, I had a wonderful time working
for Blackfriars Hall, which is the presence of the Dominican
Order in Oxford. The Latin motto for the Dominican Order is
contemplare et contemplata tradere ad aliis. This translated is: 'to
contemplate, and share with others what is contemplated'.
For the Dominicans, the contemplation that they themselves
experience, is coupled to sharing with others the fruits of their
contemplation. To contemplate deeply can bring about deep

compassion and loving kindness to others. As an example of this (Mark 1 v 35–39) we read of Jesus withdrawing, being sought out by the disciples, urged by them to come to the crowd so that He can teach and preach the Good News. The time of contemplation for the Dominicans is not a selfish activity. The time of contemplation for Jesus is not a selfish activity. The time of contemplation for us is not a selfish activity. We receive in order to give back.

The Sea of Galilee is teaming with fish because the River Jordan flows in from the north *and* out again from the south. On its journey further south, the same River Jordan flows into the Dead Sea from the north and comes to an abrupt end. Nothing flows out from it. The Dead Sea is just that, dead, no fish, no life. Jesus says in Matthew's Gospel (Matthew 7 v 16) you will know them by their fruits. What are these fruits? The fruits of time spent well, both contemplating and giving.

Thomas Merton* describes contemplation in various ways. These include an awakening suddenly, becoming aware of what is real, what is within, what is God. My understanding is that there is a slight difference of emphasis between meditation and contemplation. Meditation is looking from the outside in, in towards God. Contemplation is looking from the inside out, from what is within us, not allowing words to get in the way, and connecting with a deep silence. Contemplation is a train of thought about something. Meditation is tuning the mind to focus on something.

If we are to hear God, silent contemplation is one of the ways in which this can happen. Contemplation involves stopping, pausing, becoming alert, so that we are receptive to God.

Contemplative silence is not just an 'import' from other religions. There is a long history of Christian contemplative silence. Examples for the past include Teresa of Ávila* and John of the Cross.* St John of the Cross described contemplation as 'nothing else but a secret, peaceful and loving infusion of God, which if admitted will set the soul on fire with the spirit of love'.

It is not just the mystics of the past who have this kinship with the Divine. This connection is available and active for each and every one of us. What can happen, of course, is that the connection can become dormant. Not dormant on the part of the Divine, but on our part. We neglect our deepest being, the deepest part of us which is connected to God. And so sadly, what replaces our discovery, imagination and joy is guilt and shame. What a huge loss this is, for the Divine, and for us. The creative God is still creating, and, wants to create through us, and in us. Our contemplation of God facilitates this possibility. In the beginning God spoke into the silence. In the present, God can speak into the silence, if only we create this space and time.

Thomas Edison (1847–1931), amazing US inventor, said that genius was one per cent inspiration and ninety-nine per cent perspiration. When I was training to be a local preacher, my very wise and wonderful mentor Ron Glithero told me that my preparation for services should be a combination of inspiration and perspiration. My perspiration was to set aside time, to work through the commentaries, the newspapers and books on preaching. In some ways, he suggested, this was the easier part. My inspiration was to be setting aside time: to listen to the Divine, to receive ideas and prompts, to rely on the Divine.

We need to get a balance between contemplation and activity. At key moments in the gospel story, Jesus withdraws. It almost seems as if His time of withdrawal, for contemplation and meditation provides him with energy and the ability to deal with the key periods of activity that are about to follow. I suspect that for most of us, me included, the balance is heavily in favour of activity. I suspect for many of us the time given over to withdrawal, to contemplation is limited. Getting discernment about the right balance between activity and contemplation, and then following this discernment is quite a challenge. Even in our times of worship together, getting the right balance between activity and contemplation is quite a challenge. For many acts of worship, the time given over to contemplation is quite limited. To have an opportunity within the context of a worship service just to listen and just to be in silent presence of the Divine is quite precious.

Possibility: at some point today sit and pause for between 3 and 5 minutes. Do nothing apart from notice your breathing. How did this feel? How easy or difficult?

Doing

Come to me, all you who are weary and burdened, and I will give you rest. Take my yoke upon you and learn from me, for I am gentle and humble in heart, and you will find rest for your souls. For my yoke is easy and my burden is light.

Matthew 11 v 28–30

Then, because so many people were coming and going that they did not even have a chance to eat, he said to them, 'Come with me by yourselves to a quiet place and get some rest.'

Mark 6 v 31

Do all you can to preach the gospel, and if necessary, use words!

Francis of Assisi

Through the secret art of pausing, we develop the capacity to stop hiding, stop running away from our experience. We begin to trust in our natural intelligence, in our naturally wise heart, in our capacity to open to whatever arises.

Tara Brach

My parents would often say to me as a sullen teenager 'don't just sit there, do something'.

Mindfulness teachers, as a joke, reverse the phrase 'don't just do something, sit there'.

In the Mindfulness A Practical Guide to Finding Peace in a Frantic World course,* teachers encourage participants to practise sitting meditations at home during the week in between the weekly sessions when people meet up as a group. During my course, in one of the early feedback discussions, one of the fellow course members said that she found it really hard to find time among all her responsibilities of childcare and work to find 15 to 30 minutes to just sit, and, not do. We were all sympathetic. So, the teacher encouraged us all towards a 3-minute breathing space. When we met again the following week, the teacher asked how we had all got on. Another course member said that he found it difficult to even do this, so the teacher suggested to him that even a 30-second breathing space regularly during the day would help. The next week he came back and said that not even this had been possible, that he was too busy and stressed to even have 30 seconds. I remember being incredulous, almost cross, that he was wasting everyone's time on the course. If he could not manage even to bother with setting aside 30 seconds at some point during the day, then why was he on the course? But then I realised this was also about noticing. Noticing that he was not committed. Noticing that he was not serious. Noticing that, each week, all he wanted to do was have an audience, to inform them how busy and stressed he believed he was.

'Non-doing' is not the same as 'doing nothing'. John Kabat Zin* suggests that they could not be more different! The reason that they are so different is because the intention behind them is so different. Non-doing is intentional and difficult. Doing nothing is not intentional and easy (for many people). Non-doing requires that time is set aside. In the way that you might set aside time for the gym or going to the pub, you need to set aside time for non-doing. When talking about mindfulness with others, I have often heard the reaction that there simply is 'not enough time in the day' for a time of non-doing. But the attitude being expressed here suggests that the speaker hasn't recognised non-doing for what it is and what the ultimate benefits might be. Non-doing is about cultivating an attitude of letting things be and letting them unfold. Non-doing meditation is a time when we are not seeking to make things perfectly calm, perfectly serene, perfectly stress free. Rather, it is a chance to discern, to become aware that things are the way they are. So non-doing is just being in the present and not wishing it was somehow different. This setting aside time for non-doing cultivates more effective doing for the rest of the day. This is because it allows a person to be more present to the other parts of their day. Being more to be more present means being more effective.

For most of my working life, I worked in the University of Oxford. This is a place and environment which attracts more than its fair share of driven people. I am guessing that the percentage of driven, doing people would be far higher than the national average. For many students and staff, the culture of doing, succeeding, impressing others, is heightened and intensified. The symptoms of the very driven life are awful. I therefore witnessed, among students, staff and academics an inability to enjoy the success of being at a world top 10 University. It was sad and unfortunate that, for some, it reached the point of anxiety, depression and severe eating disorders.

In my latter years of working there, mindfulness was introduced as one of the mechanisms to help staff and students to cope. As part of my work in University, I also worked with those training for ordained ministry. Among these people, many found themselves 'doing, doing, doing'. One was working 70 hours per week as well as the training – and it is no surprise that this person burnt out and never made it through.

As I write this book, I have just given up employment to begin early retirement. It is very interesting to make some observations as I seek to settle into this different pattern of life and lifestyle. In my early days, I noticed a sense of guilt – for not working any longer. Others find a great change in self-worth because their worth came from the status of the role or job. Among the Christian community, many are driven on by doing, any kind of doing – preaching, organising attending meetings, pastoral visiting, any kind of doing just to avoid being. Maybe it is time for non-doing as part of your day?

Possibility: ponder on the difference between 'non-doing' and 'doing nothing'. Does an opportunity arise for non-doing sometime today?

Eyes

Your eye is the lamp of your body. When your eyes are healthy, your whole body also is full of light.
Luke 11 v 34

But blessed are your eyes because they see, and your ears because they hear.
Matthew 13 v 16

Jesus himself came up and walked along with them; but they were kept from recognizing him. Then their eyes were opened and they recognized him, and he disappeared from their sight.
Luke 24 v 16, 31

The things we see every day, are the things we never see at all.
GK Chesterton

There is nothing like looking, if you want to find something.
JRR Tolkien

In the twenty-first century there is so much more visual stuff bombarding our eyes. Electronic screens of all types: phones, tablets, laptops, TV screens are all pummelling our eyes and our minds with so many images. One piece of health advice often given in health magazines and books is not to look at a phone screen for about an hour before bedtime, as the quality of the blue light somehow stimulates the mind and has a negative impact on the ability to get to sleep. Our eyes are so much more than sophisticated video cameras. The images are, in the most incredible way, transformed into so much more by our brains, our imagination, our night-time dreams, our hearts. It is said that our eyes are the window of the soul.

When your eyes are open, observant, seeing, then your whole body your whole person is made of light. Eyes are turned outwards towards what is around us. We are created as outward looking people, towards the nature surrounding us. It is interesting that for most people on holiday, their eyes do seem to be more open and more receptive to what is around. Because there is novelty, the eyes take in more. Buildings, flowers, water, all attracting our eyes. In our everyday lives when not on holiday, there is of course still so much to see. If only we are able to slow down, to notice, to have a different attitude to what is around us, then our 'holiday eyes' might still function. During the coronavirus lockdown, I went on the same circular cycle ride many times for our permitted one period of exercise each day. And each day, was amazed by what I hadn't seen before – beautiful trees, changing colours and shapes each day. This provided a wonderful opportunity for attentive seeing.

What you see, how you see, determines what you are and what you will be. When a bird comes into the garden to feed there are different ways to see that bird. An initial reaction might be that 'it's only a sparrow', not very colourful, not very interesting, not as attractive as a goldfinch; in fact, I won't bother giving it my time or attention. But there is an alternative! However, the alternative requires a momentary pause. And in that pause, you might recollect that the small, not very colourful bird has intrinsic beauty and form. And as you pause, and notice, you begin to see the shape, and the colour, and the movement of the bird. To do all this requires that you are present. Were you willing to give attention, and perhaps even recall that even sparrows are appreciated and significant to God (Matthew 10 v 29–31)?

In the early episodes of the most recent *Sherlock* series on television, Sherlock Holmes (played by Benedict Cumberbatch) criticises Dr John Watson for his lack of observation and noticing.

Mindfulness can help improve seeing, by being more attentive, by giving space and time. It is through this same kind of process that mindfulness can improve hearing, through attentive listening. Some mindfulness practitioners suggest a practical exercise which involves looking intently or what they call 'attentive seeing'. The exercise requires the observer to look at a specific thing or in a specific way. So, one example is to look at one tree for five or ten minutes. Another example is to select one square foot of the ground in front of you and then give your visual attention to that for five or ten minutes. This kind of exercise is really interesting and informative. It is interesting to notice just how many times your mind is somewhere else, distracted, planning, worrying about something past or something future. Ten minutes is not a very long time, five minutes even less, and yet for some people doing this exercise, for this short period of time can seem like an eternity.

Jesus said, 'I am the light of the world' (John 8 v 12). There is a beautiful painting by Holman Hunt called *The Light of the World* (one copy in Keble College, Oxford and the other copy in St Pauls Cathedral). The painting is one of my very favourites. It is beautifully constructed, depicting the verse where Jesus says 'behold I stand at the door and knock' (Revelation 3 v 20). On the face of Jesus is quite an amazing expression, which is not angry but sympathetic and understanding to the people on the other side of the door on which he knocks. The quality of the light in the painting which comes from a lantern held in the hand of Jesus is also quite amazing. If only people would open the door, which can only be done from the inside, because there is no handle on the outside, then they would see Jesus. If only the disciples would open their eyes (Mark 8 v 17–18), then they would see Jesus, would see the Light of the World.

Catherine of Siena* wrote that the more you see, the more you can love. The more that you can see about yourself, then hopefully, the more that you can love about yourself. And then, wonderfully, because of this, there is the potential to love others and to love God more.

Possibility: spend five minutes focussing on one particular scene, tree, piece of ground in front of you. If a thought distraction comes along, smile, and return your focus. Enjoy the sensations.

Ego

Jesus, who, being in very nature God, did not consider equality with God something to be used to His own advantage; rather, He made himself nothing by taking the very nature of a servant, being made in human likeness. And being found in appearance as a man, He humbled himself by becoming obedient to death, even death on a cross!
Philippians 2 v 5–8

What good is it for someone to gain the whole world, and yet lose or forfeit their very self?
Luke 9 v 26

For whoever wants to save their life will lose it, but whoever loses their life for me and for the gospel will save it.
Mark 8 v 35

All you need to know and observe in yourself is this: whenever you feel superior, or inferior, to anyone, that is the ego in you.
Eckhart Tolle

One may understand the cosmos, but never the ego; the self is more distant than any star.
GK Chesterton

In many places we read and hear that our ego is shaped and affected by our early years. Shaped by the ideas of others and the expectations that were projected upon us, especially by parents, but also by teachers and peers. And in a very complex way, these are mixed together to create either stability and a healthy balance for us, or, instability and an unhealthy balance. When I was a child, my mother would often tell me that I was the best in the class. For a while, I believed this *might* be true when things were going well at junior school. But eventually, I could see, very clearly, that this was not the case! And it created a dilemma in my mind, and it was very confusing for my ego. The ego can at times get very busy with the hyperactivity of comparing ourselves with others. Sometimes we compare ourselves to others, feeling superior in order to make ourselves feel better – but how long does this last? Time spent comparing ourselves unfavourably with others, as being inferior, can be very destructive and detrimental to our well-being. The Facebook generation knows a lot about this. The ego can create and form a very false sense of self.

I once went to a talk about 'seeking to be average'. I wonder what answer you might get, if you were to ask Roger Federer or Lionel Messi whether they wanted to be average in their sport? I think we can all guess the answer. Who wants to be average? Well actually, it is perhaps an enormous relief to be just average. Average means not having to strive to be better than everyone else. Average means just that, that you are more able than some people and less able than some other people. And once you can arrive at that happy place, it really becomes less important how many people you are more able or less able than!

As I approached early retirement, many people who had already taken retirement were very keen to tell me about how very busy they had become since retiring. One of the oft repeated mantras was that 'since I have retired, I am so busy that I don't know how I managed to fit work in'. I came to recognise that for many people their ego demands that 'I am useful', 'I am needed', 'I am popular'. It is interesting how the ego gets to work, and how this work skews what people say and feel about themselves. The ego can create a false self, which is defensive, anxious and fearful, a self which needs to have a role that is recognised by others. The poet Angelus Silesius* wrote, 'A rose is but a rose, it blooms because it blooms; it thinks not of itself, nor asks if it is seen.'

When we are trying to meditate, the ego can get busy very quickly. Under these circumstances, seeking to fight the ego is impossible. Other strategies are required. And one strategy that may work is simply noticing – noticing what the ego is wanting to do, where the ego is trying to take you. And most of all, remembering that we are not our ego, which can build masks and walls and conceal our real selves. We do need to have a healthy ego. An unhealthy ego causes distress to ourselves, and also distresses those around us. Richard Rohr* suggests that the anxious, insecure ego also hijacks the mind.

Each one of us attracts so many labels: mother, dentist, priest, cleaner, professor. And all of these labels are quickly used by others to define us, often wrongly. A more subtle set of labels are also attached to us: clever, beautiful, introvert, loser, and these more subtle labels, likewise, are used by others to wrongly define us. This second set of labels are very subjective. Clever in comparison to who? Beautiful in comparison to? And then we have labels which are prejudiced, discriminatory, hateful: Jew. black, woman. These labels and prejudices can be so incredibly unhelpful and destructive. The ego uses this structure that we build around ourselves, and it starts to happen from a young age. How we present ourselves to others, how we protect ourselves, and how we validate ourselves are put into place as we grow. But the danger in all of this for all of us is that we separate ourselves from each other, and even worse than this, we separate ourselves from our true self. Our ego thoughts, which can come and go, can nevertheless imprison us. Especially when the inner voice (inner critic) incessantly chatters on.

Jesus knows what it is like for us. He knows how difficult life is! How the ego is unrelentingly busy.

Mindfulness can help us let go of the ego and can combine with grace towards each one of us becoming a new creation. We are reminded (Philippians 2 v 5–8) that Jesus humbled himself and emptied Himself. This does not mean he emptied his mind of everything, rather that he emptied his mind of the unhelpful worldly things which were distractions. And here Jesus provides us with a model for our lives.

Possibility: at some point today, as you meet someone, how might you label them or compare yourself with them (positively or negatively)? How does this labelling or comparing make you feel?

Freedom

Now the Lord is the Spirit, and where the Spirit of the Lord is, there is freedom.
2 Corinthians 3 v 17

I do not understand what I do. For what I want to do I do not do, but what I hate I do.
For I do not do the good I want to do, but the evil I do not want to do—this I keep on doing.
Romans 7 v 15, 19

You, my brothers and sisters, were called to be free.
But do not use your freedom to indulge the flesh, rather, serve one another humbly in love.
Galatians 5 v 13

You can never be free if you have an ego to defend.
Anthony de Mello

It is for freedom that Christ has set us free.
Paul to the Galatians

Like many people in the country, I have completely given up making New Year's Resolutions.

The last time I made a resolution was years ago. The resolution was that I should go swimming 20 times in the coming year. Rather than have the pressure of going every week, 20 times was about once every two weeks, which I thought was easily achievable. At the end of the year the number of times that I went swimming was totalled up. It wasn't a difficult calculation. It was a very round number – precisely zero! I had the freedom to go any week. I also had the freedom to not go!

In more recent times, and since coming to mindfulness, I start the year with an intention. Not a resolution, not a phrase or command to bind me, to take away freedom. No, an intention gives freedom – freedom to explore something different. And the intention is to work with a single word for the year. The best example that comes to mind is recently working with the word 'should'. Wow – what a word! Noticing the number of times I used the word verbally, and, the number of times a silent voice in my thoughts said should (do better etc.), was quite surprising and quite sobering! Just how many times this word arose was affecting freedom.

The freedom that mindfulness seeks to offer is the same freedom that Jesus seeks to offer us.

The freedom of letting things be, the freedom not to wish things were different, or otherwise. And the freedom to be present in the presence of God. Through mindful awareness, we can become cognisant of who we really are. And the more we are able to exercise this freedom, the more the possibility to have freedom to become all that God would have us to be. The freedom to have abundant life (zest) which Jesus wishes us to have.

I have just read *The Librarian of Auschwitz*, which is a horrifying account of the Nazi inhumanity to Jews. But the novel is also a story of hope, and a message of freedom, the freedom of minds despite the horrific incarceration endured by millions of Jews. Nelson Mandela provides us with a wonderful example in his autobiography *The Long Walk to Freedom*. At the heart of the book, at the heart of a life lived, is forgiveness and compassion. And this forgiveness and compassion provides freedom. Jesus says to us 'you should know the truth, and the truth shall set you free' (John 8 v 32). Mindfulness helps us come to terms with the things that enslave us and take away our freedom. These are often distorted replays of past events, and their contorted implications. Once we start to recognise thoughts as just thoughts, and, that we are not our thoughts, then we can start on our own long walk to freedom.

On our walk to freedom, mindfulness can help us in how we respond in any given situation. Mindfulness can help make longer the momentary pause between a stimulus that we receive and the reaction to that stimulus. This momentary pause is a real freedom. We can be free to choose good or bad; the left fork or the right fork; the carrying on as always or making a *metanoia* change. We have freedom, and that freedom, is just between Jesus and me. Once we can all understand this, once we all realise how free from their judgement we are, it is so liberating, so wonderful, so life giving.

God allows us choice every day, every hour, every moment. To make the choice to do God's will is an act of freedom. The choices that we make in this freedom have consequences for ourselves and for those around us. Our freedom to act like the Good Samaritan or not partly depends on how we organise ourselves. The freedom to stop and offer assistance is determined by whether we allow sufficient slack and leeway in our lives? Whether we allow sufficient time to stop and help rather than being pressed by an ever-insistent diary. The diary may be full of worthy events or church activities – but to have time and space really matters. For it allows us rather to see things more clearly to be more proactive.

We have the freedom from should and ought and must. Do we have the freedom to be open and curious about mindfulness or not? I would encourage you all to say YES, I would like to have all these freedoms. YES, I want to have the abundant life (zest) that Jesus offers.

Possibility: when water turns to ice, it loses its fluidity. Is there an unhelpful concept that you hold on to, that has frozen in your mind, causing it to lose fluidity?

Forgiveness
(including the parable of the Prodigal Son)

But while he was still a long way off, his father saw him and was filled with compassion for him; he ran to his son, threw his arms around him and kissed him.
Luke 15 v 20 (from passage of v 11–30)

Therefore, my friends, I want you to know that through Jesus, the forgiveness of sins is proclaimed to you.
Acts 13 v 38

And Peter came to Jesus and asked, 'Lord how many times shall I forgive my brother or sister who sins against me, up to 7 times?' Jesus answered, 'I tell you, not seven times but seventy times seven.'
Matthew 18 v 21–22

We all agree that forgiveness is a beautiful idea, until we have to practise it.
CS Lewis

Whatever our religion, we know that if we really want to love, we must first learn to forgive before anything else.
Mother Teresa

Max Lucado* wrote: 'If our greatest need had been information, God would have sent an educator. If our greatest need had been technology, God would have sent us a scientist. If our greatest need had been money, God would have sent us an economist. But since our greatest need was forgiveness, God sent us a Saviour.' Forgiveness is a chance to start again, for the person receiving the forgiveness, but also, for the person carrying out the act of forgiveness. Desmond Tutu says that, 'Forgiveness says you are given another chance to make a new beginning.'

This is clearly illustrated in the parable which appears in Luke chapter 15. From this brilliant parable (Luke 15 v 11–30), called the parable of the 'Prodigal Son', there is much to be learned about forgiveness, but also about the spiritual life and the mindful life. This is a parable, an illustrative story, about life being experienced. In each of the parables, Jesus delivers a punchline, an unexpected twist to the story, a turning upside down of what the hearer might have expected to hear. The parable stories and illustrations paint pictures so clearly about what goes on in many lives – mistakes, regret, forgiveness, envy, annoyance, love. This particular parable, longer than most, does this more than most. Perhaps the best way to gain the maximum understanding from this parable, is to consider each of the main characters – the father, the older son, and the younger son (who is called the prodigal son).

In the parable, the father has every reason to be aggrieved. Reading it now, in the UK in the 2020s, it is quite difficult to understand culturally that he has been treated badly, very, very badly by his younger son. The way in which the younger son asks for his inheritance is effectively saying to the father, 'I wish you were dead!' This is the first shock in the parable. Despite all of this, and almost incredibly, the father is a wonderful example of somebody who personifies forgiveness. And as the story progresses, we are able to see that one of the reasons he is able to do this is by living in the present moment. In spite of the despicable actions of his younger son, he is there waiting each day, hoping for his return. When his son appears on the horizon, because the father is in the present moment and awake, he opens his arms wide and welcomes the younger son with gratitude and forgiveness. Sermons in church will concentrate on this parable as a story of forgiveness, and it is in huge measure. But it is more. It also provides an example of how the father is able to forgive because he is mindfully there and present.

The younger son, the prodigal son, goes away and squanders all his inheritance. The point in the story where we find him, a Jew, among the pigs, is another culturally shocking moment in the parable. And then, even more culturally shocking, is that the prodigal son is eating the scraps the pigs leave behind! Things could hardly be worse. But then he comes to his senses. He realises with great clarity, that things can be different. He realises that even the servants of his father have a very much better life than he is experiencing. In this one *metanoia* (see change) moment he comes to his senses. He makes the step from mindless to mindful, from asleep to awake. In this one, present, *metanoia* moment he realises it could be no worse. (In this one, present, *metanoia* moment **you** may notice that things could be very significantly better.) And when he comes to this moment, (perhaps epiphany), he comes to the present in both his mind and his body. He takes action. He walks home, one mindful step at a time.

And finally, in contrast, the older son is portrayed as not living in the present moment. He is miserable and grumpy. When the younger son comes back home this all comes to the surface in the parable so brilliantly told by Jesus. The older son looks backwards and forwards. He looks back to all the time that he spent at home while the prodigal son squandered his inheritance. He also projects forward to the time when he believes his portion of the inheritance will be diminished by the return of the prodigal son. As a consequence, the older son is not able to be present, to celebrate, to be joyful. The reader can only imagine that if the older son has no change of heart, no moment of clarity, no forgiveness, then he will live the rest of his life in misery and resentment. Mentally, he will be living as the younger son had lived physically in the worst of conditions among the pigs.

The parable is also about coming alive again, coming home

coming back to love. How unhappy and resentful is the person who cannot forgive her/himself. How unhappy and resentful is the person who cannot forgive others. How trapped in the past is the person who cannot forgive. Nelson Mandela realised this as he left Robben Island. The older son is trapped and needs to understand that he must forgive his younger brother. Then he would have a chance like the father and the younger son to have abundant life (zest).

Possibility: at some point today, can you forgive someone for one small thing. It might be yourself, a friend or family member, or a work colleague. Notice afterwards how it feels.

Getting There

We made slow headway for many days and had difficulty arriving off Cnidus.

Acts 27 v 7

Perhaps I will stay with you for a while, or even spend the winter, so that you can help me on my journey, wherever I go.

1 Corinthians 16 v 6

The hurrier I go, the behinder I get.

Lewis Carroll

Success is a journey, not a destination. It requires constant effort, vigilance and re-evaluation.

Mark Twain

Daniel Batson and his supervisor John Darley, behavioural scientists at Princetown University, conducted an experiment which was written up as a paper in 1973 about social behaviour.

The study set out to consider whether it was the disposition of people, or their situations, which caused people to act in a particular way? The study was carried out amongst a group of students at Princeton who were studying to be priests. Half the students were asked to prepare a talk about career prospects, half the students were asked to prepare a talk about the Good Samaritan story – so not only priests in training, but priests actively considering the act of compassion carried out by the Samaritan in the parable told by Jesus (see also compassion). In the experiment, the student priests were told that they needed to walk to a nearby building to give their talk. The really important part about the study was that the participant students were randomly split up into three groups. Group 1 was told that they had plenty of time and they were early; Group 2 that they were on time but they should make their way over to the other building; Group 3 that they were running a bit late and that they needed to move quite fast.

Batson and Darley had arranged, unbeknown to the students, for an actor to be lying on the ground, apparently mugged and unwell, on the route between the two buildings. The students had to pass by the actor to get to their presentations. The experiment found that their behaviour was not significantly affected by what the subject of the talk was about. However, the behaviour of the students in the three groups was found to be significantly different, despite the fact they were all on the same course with an intention to become priests. Sixty-three per cent of the students from Group 1 (the 'early' group) stopped to help the stranger. Forty-five per cent of the students from Group 2 (the 'on-time' group) stopped to help the stranger. And only 10% of the students from Group 3 (the 'late' group) stopped. The researchers concluded that it was the perceived time available to the students, rather than their own innate disposition, which really mattered.

This outcome is of interest and has implications for us all. We can create conditions when we have insufficient time, insufficient journey time, insufficient preparation time. In Alice in Wonderland, the White Rabbit says: 'I'm late, I'm late, for a very important date. No time for hellos or goodbyes, I'm late, I'm late, I'm late.' The result is that 'getting there' becomes more important than how we get there. But our journeys are so much about getting there! One person I know used to have to travel to the north east of England regularly, and for him, it was about 'getting on the motorway and putting my foot down'. The actual journey was just an impediment, a delay, something to be endured rather than enjoyed. So many of our journeys are about habit, what the psychologist call autopilot. So, we are not really being present to the journey itself, to seeing what beauty might be on offer. Rather it is about getting from A to B, home to work, work to home.

When I was working, my commute to work was about 40 minutes in duration. For many people this would be a blissful commute. The first part was a 30-minute walk in rural West Oxfordshire, along the edge of the Blenheim Palace estate. This was followed by a 10-minute train ride into the city of Oxford. And then, the third part a gentle 10-minute walk from Oxford station to my workplace.

I would regularly use the 30-minute walk down to the station to measure the busyness of my mind. About 10 minutes before arriving at the station, there is a railway bridge to be crossed. I used to use this bridge as a landmark, in particular to determine whether I had been noticing sights and sounds around me or had just been lost in thoughts. In my early days of having come to mindfulness, all too often I would be very much lost in thoughts about work and other anxieties. But as the weeks and months went on the situation improved. I had started noticing sights and sounds, and on good days, well before the bridge. This is not in any way to be boastful or self-congratulatory, but to help identify just how difficult it is to form good habits. During the third part of the commute, the shorter walk in through the city of Oxford, one thing I tried to do, suggested by the teacher on my original 8-week course, was to look up. And by this I don't mean just eye level, but to really look up. It is amazing what you can see. Two particular favourites, were the maple trees by the Business School and the Conker tree by the history faculty, through the seasons and in different lights. But also worth mentioning was graffiti high on buildings near the roof tops.

For each one of us, the days will vary greatly. Sometimes the journey may be more mindful. Sometimes the intention of 'getting there' may predominate. But rather than be disappointed, or judgemental, it is always a case of accepting what is.

Possibility: if you are able to, go for a short circular local walk, with no purpose or target. Just enjoy the activity of walking, your feet on the ground, the air on your face, and the knowledge that you are 'not seeking to get there'.

Gratitude

Then he took the seven loaves and the fish, and when he had given thanks...
Matthew 15 v 36

Give thanks in all circumstances; for this is God's will for you in Christ Jesus.
1 Thessalonians 5 v 18

I thank Christ Jesus our Lord, who has given me strength, that he considered me trustworthy, appointing me to his service.
1 Timothy 1 v 12

We must find time to stop and thank the people who make a difference in our lives.
John F Kennedy

Piglet noticed that even though he had a very small heart, it could hold rather a large amount of gratitude.
AA Milne

There are many studies and articles about what makes people happy. They seem to indicate that wealth, financial reward and riches do not really do the trick. Television programmes, magazine articles and books seem to indicate that people who win very large amounts of money on the lottery are not grateful and generally not happy. My experience of a wide range of people in the city of Oxford, the University of Oxford, in churches and in workplaces suggests to me that gratitude does not bear any real correlation to material well-being, position or circumstances. If anything, there might even be a small inverse correlation! Gratitude, however, does seem to have a strong correlation with attitude. Listening to the interviews on *Desert Island Discs* with various people from differing backgrounds, is very informative. What often emerges is a strong sense of gratitude, to parents and teachers, who inspire and encourage those on the programme to go on with their chosen vocation or skill.

Being grateful takes us outside of ourselves. What can we be grateful for? We can be grateful to other people for support and help, grateful for companionship, grateful for small things in life, grateful for nature around us, grateful for food, grateful to God for many blessings. And when we express gratitude to someone else this has a double benefit. The receiver of the gratitude gets a blessing but, at the same time, the giver of the gratitude gets a blessing. Occasionally, a person who witnesses expression of gratitude from one person to another also gets a blessing. Gratitude can be shown in so many different ways. The most common way probably is verbally, but it can also be a simple hug, smile, a thumbs-up, a text or an email. So many different ways in which we can all make a difference to ourselves and to those around us by expressing gratitude.

Gratitude is an essential part of mindfulness. Gratitude is an essential part of life! My own background is one of starting from poor beginnings. And I think these poor beginnings have helped imbue a sense of gratitude throughout my life. But mindfulness has helped me much more. It has helped me to have a real gratitude for each and every day. And my gratitude is not for material things, but for conversations, interactions, small acts of kindness, sight, smell, hearing and many, many other things. When Jesus breaks bread he gives thanks. Here we have an example of Jesus being grateful in the simplest of situations.

Being grateful can become a habit. Often when we talk about habits these have negative connotations, e.g., smoking or eating too much. In contrast, the habit of being grateful has many positive connotations. And unlike many habits, it is one that you can enjoy as many times a day as you wish. Amazingly, the more that you have this habit the better it is for you. And if you are able to live more and more in the present moment, then it is possible to be grateful in the present moment and the now. There are lots of present moments in each and every day.

Just as mindfulness can be hard, needs practice, and can meet resistance in our own mind, so sometimes, showing gratitude can be hard and can meet resistance in our mind. Gratitude can form an antidote to feelings of not having enough, to judgemental thoughts, to unhelpful comparisons with others. It can be that if we take a moment to be grateful, then in that moment and for that moment, temptations to have these negative thoughts and emotions can be suspended. Whatever your situation, wherever you are, however hard your life might have been in the past or might be at the moment, each and every one of us can be grateful. We can all be grateful for each and every breath that we have, as each breath gives us nourishment and vitality. And as we take every single breath it is possible for us to be grateful for being alive, and being alive to the presence of God. This breath-by-breath gratitude can improve our emotional and mental health.

The word 'thank' appears 64 times in the New Testament and 133 in the Old Testament. Jesus gives thanks before the last supper, the raising of Lazarus and in many other situations. A practical tip for showing gratitude is to pray very short and immediate prayers – to give thanks in the moment rather than trying to remember things at the end of a tiring day. We can of course follow up at the end of the day as we deliberately bring back to mind, say, five things that we are grateful for that have happened that day.

Possibility: perhaps say a short thank you prayer 5 times during the remainder of today.

Happiness

For example, verse 8: Happy are the pure in heart, for they will see God.
Matthew various verses in Ch 5

Is not life more than food, and the body more than clothes?
Matthew 6 v 25

Though you have not seen him, you love him; and even though you do not see him now, you believe in him and are filled with an inexpressible and glorious joy.
1 Peter 1 v 8

You don't have to add anything in order to be happy, you've got to drop something.
Anthony de Mello

Be happy in the moment, that's enough. Each moment is all we need not more.
Mother Teresa

There is a beautiful book of conversations between the Dalai Lama* and Archbishop Desmond Tutu* which is called *The Book of Joy*. The subtitle of the book is 'Lasting Happiness in a Changing World'. On page 14, the Dalai Lama is asked the question, 'What is the purpose of life?' And the reply given is, 'I believe that the purpose of life is to find happiness.' But the book acknowledges that these feelings of happiness are hard to find, like a butterfly that lands on us and then flies and flutters away. There are so many things that undermine our joy and happiness that we create ourselves because of the negative tendencies of our minds. Mathieu Ricard* in his book *Happiness: A Guide to*

Developing Life's Most Important Skill, defines happiness as 'a deep sense of flourishing that arises from an exceptionally healthy mind. This is not for me a pleasurable feeling, fleeting emotion or a mood, but an optimal state of being'.

God wants us to be happy! I am sure of this. God is unchangeable. Our neighbours and our work colleagues are changeable. It doesn't matter how we appear to our neighbours – we will not bring long-term and deep happiness by pleasing our neighbours because they are fickle and changeable. It does matter how we are with God. God can and will bring long-term and deep happiness. And yet, sometimes deep happiness can be elusive.

In the interaction between Jesus and a woman at the well (John 4 v 9–29), He identifies that she has been married five times and the man she is currently living with is not her husband. Is she happy? It does not seem so. Happiness seems to be eluding her – she seems to be making the same mistakes time after time. And in her life of drudgery, she returns to the well day after day to fill the water pot. Jesus offers her living water. Jesus offers her something different and special. Jesus offers her happiness. William Hartley, known as the founder of Hartley Jams, who came from a Methodist family, and who was a committed Christian throughout his life, was known for his incredible energy and philanthropic activities (supporting education, hospitals, workers' conditions). Hartley once said: 'Thank God, happiness is from within and not from without. It is what a person is, and not what a person has.'

It would seem some of our happiness depends on how we come to terms with the past. The past can be wonderful or difficult, and this can have a significant bearing on present happiness. But the extent to which we are able to live in the present moment has an impact on this. And in coming to terms with the past and the present, forgiving others, and forgiving oneself, can also make a significant difference.

Gross National Happiness is an index that has guided the government of Bhutan since 2008. It now forms part of their constitution. What they do is value collective happiness by placing weighting on certain aspects of life. If only more countries could follow this lead! For many of us it may be difficult to change the world in a significant way, although we are all able to make small contributions in the life situations that we have been placed into. However difficult it may be for us to change the world; it is always possible to change the way that we look at it. This is very much what mindfulness is about. Happiness is a way of interpreting the world. A way to change your level of happiness is not by changing the actual circumstances, but by changing the way that you look at these circumstances, changing the way you interpret things. In turn this might result in perhaps changing your values and your goals. It is not so much what happens *to* us as to what happens *in* us that counts. Bound up with our happiness is humility. If we are truly humble, then we have nothing to lose and nothing to gain and so happiness is much more achievable.

In his ministry, Jesus turned so many things upside down. If we look at the Sermon on the Mount (Matthew 5), Jesus repeatedly uses the word 'blessed' or 'happy', depending on which translation you use. Happy or blessed are people on earth and in heaven i.e., we enjoy the first fruits now and the full harvest later in heaven. The Greek word for blessed or happy being used here is *Makarios*, a joy which has its secret within itself, a joy which is independent of chances and changes in life. This passage does not say blessed are the brilliant people, blessed are those with a PhD in theology, the pushy people, the uncaring people. No! It says blessed and happy are those who are ready to accept grace and love, people who are poor in spirit, gentle, peacemakers etc. Later in the Sermon on the Mount (Matthew 6 v 25–31), Jesus identifies that this happiness springs from living in the present, not being anxious about tomorrow, recognising our own worth and our worth to God. What an amazing and captivating passage of teaching which turns things upside down and helps us gain perspective of what really matters.

Possibility: spend a few moments now giving attention to your face and body... smile to yourself, move your shoulders round a couple of times and settle into a comfortable position, open your eyes to surroundings, take a couple of deep breaths, and smile again to yourself. Repeat as many times as you wish today!

Humility

Jesus called the Twelve and said, "Anyone who wants to be first must be the very last, and the servant of all."
Mark 9 v 35

I am not saying this because I am in need, for I have learned to be content whatever the circumstances.
Philippians 4 v 11

But the Lord said to me 'My grace is sufficient for you, for my power is made perfect in weakness.' Therefore, I will boast all the more gladly about my weaknesses, so that Christ's power may rest on me. That is why, for Christ's sake, I delight in weaknesses, in insults, in hardships, in persecutions, in difficulties. For when I am weak, then I am strong.
2 Cor 12 v 9–10

Pride makes us artificial; humility makes us real.
Thomas Merton

In the course of my life, I have often had to eat my words, And I must confess, that I have always found it a wholesome diet.
Winston Churchill

Winston Churchill also said that humility is not thinking less of ourselves, but thinking about ourselves less of the time. This is the key balance between ego and humility. The rule of Benedict speaks much about humility. And in the words of Augustine, humility is the first thing the second thing and the third thing. Humility is a little bit elusive – just when you think you have it you have lost it! Humility is about putting our ego to the side.

Humility is powerful and positive, not weedy and negative. In David Copperfield, Uriah Heep has a false and insincere humility, referring often to his own *'umblness.* Humility needs strength and courage. It is not an attribute for weak and passive people, but for everybody. Humility requires for us to be in the present moment, not seeking to reflect in the glories that we once had, nor seeking to anticipate what advancement or glory might come in the future.

Humility involves accepting information about yourself. And this acceptance of information needs to be carried out with a 'beginner's mind'. And, like when you are a beginner at anything, there is much to learn, mistakes to notice and to learn from. An infant when learning to walk will make mistakes and totter and fall. The infant could say to her/himself 'I am too important to be falling over and making a fool of myself like this' or could smile to her/himself, get up and try again. When people come to play pickleball for the first time, there are some who have such good hand/eye co-ordination that they take to it quickly. Others struggle with the bounce of the ball (lower than tennis). For the new person at pickleball there can be two ways forward: Humility says okay – I need to learn. Lack of humility – I am not coming back! This humility can apply to the whole of life, whatever age, whatever you are trying to do. And, if applied to the whole of life, how much more zest (abundant life) is available.

Mistakes are an important part of learning. Some years ago, I read of a pottery experiment. In the experiment, the potters were split into two groups. The first group of Potters were asked to produce one perfect item. This first group could take as long as they wished to produce this item. The second group were allowed to have several goes, and to make mistakes, throw away some clay and just do the best they could within the time available. It doesn't take much imagination to work out which group produced the better results, because by allowing the second group to make mistakes they were able to improve their technique and end up with a better finished article even though they were not seeking for it to be perfect.

Mindfulness is valuable in discovering more about yourself. More self-awareness facilitates noticing our own strengths (to be grateful for) but also our own weaknesses (also to be grateful for!). Awareness about our strengths and weaknesses gives us more challenges for a realistic and honest acceptance of ourselves. It increases our chances to recognise our mistakes, and, perhaps even sometimes to apologise from time to time. There is a very big difference between humility, and, telling ourselves that we are failures. For humility to flourish and develop, it will involve self-forgetfulness. Self-forgetfulness involves letting go of our previous mistakes and not replaying them in our minds time after time. Lack of humility is saying to God 'we can do it' or 'I'm okay, thanks, and have got my own strength to do it'. Humility is the opposite, it is not a self-effort, but seeking the presence and strength of God in every aspect of our lives.

Mindfulness can lead us to a greater and clearer understanding of humility. This humility is contrary to the current social media driven world of seeking to become .... (insert your own word), and seeking to project self-imagery which is anything but humble. The social media way of praising oneself with words and images, based on illusions and ambitions that are unreal, is not the way of humility. Humility is one of the key aspects of Christian discipleship and spirituality. Mindfulness teaches us that a vital part of humility is accepting oneself. The practice of non-judging helps with this self-acceptance. Self-acceptance is something that can be practised and learned. And more self-acceptance can in turn have a beneficial effect on the acceptance of other people.

Possibility: reflect upon and consider the phrase 'the truly humble person never knows that they are humble'.

Interconnectedness

I say to every one of you: Do not think of yourself more highly than you ought, but rather think of yourself with sober judgment, in accordance with the faith God has distributed to each of you. For just as each of us has one body with many members, and these members do not all have the same function, so in Christ we, though many, form one body, and each member belongs to all the others.
Romans 12 v 3–5

There are different kinds of gifts, but the same Spirit distributes them. There are different kinds of service, but the same Lord.
1 Corinthians 12 v 4–5

Just as a body, though one, has many parts, but all its many parts form one body, so it is with Christ.
1 Corinthians 12 v 12

Compassion is the keen awareness of the interdependence of all things.
Thomas Merton

In our interconnected world, we must learn to feel enlarged, not threatened by difference.
Jonathan Sacks

When looking at my family tree, I discovered that my ancestors of the seventeenth and eighteenth centuries ventured little distance from the village of Newent in Gloucestershire. In Newent, there are many records of the births, marriages and deaths of a family that mainly were ordinary farm labourers. Similarly,

Jesus ventured little distance from the Galilee region of Israel. Jerusalem was two days' walk away. And in this very localised environment, during His ministry, Jesus made connections, and made these connections to people in a deep way. He listened well. He noticed well. Because of this, he asked deep questions. Through this listening, noticing and questioning, he sensitively connected with people and was able to help them and also heal them exactly where they were in that moment of their lives. And because of all this, His interactions with people were really meaningful. Think of the woman at the well (John 4 v 10–11) with her very mixed-up life of multiple relationships – to which Jesus carefully listened, noticed, questioned and then of course healed at the very deepest level. What an example for us. What a model for us to follow. How much more will we be as people if we are able to do this?

In complete contrast to the seventeenth and eighteenth centuries, it is interesting how the country has changed over the last 30 or 40 years. We have become significantly more geographically mobile, both nationally and also internationally. During these decades, I believe we have become more individualistic, and less community orientated. 'I am, because I want.' 'I am, because I can buy.' But there is an entirely different way to think about personal identity and how we are in relation to other people. The African philosophy of *ubuntu* is one in which your sense of self is shaped by your relationships with other people. It is a philosophy, a way of understanding life, that begins with the concept that 'I am' only because 'we are'. So *ubuntu* means that each and every person is a person through other people. Being, thinking, saying, acting, doing are all collective. Therefore, all saying, acting, doing which might harm or cause suffering to other people will ultimately cause harm and suffering to ourselves: 'I am because we are.' But this philosophy of *ubuntu* extends not only to other people, but to all sentient beings. 'I am because we are' extends to the nature around us and the sentient beings in this natural world. Desmond Tutu describes *ubuntu* in this way: 'A person is a person through other persons.' We come into the world through another person, we are nurtured and supported through other people, we learn our skills of talking, walking, writing, and behaviour through other people. We need others. Not just in babyhood and childhood, but throughout our lives.

It is always good to remember our interdependence with the community around us. As our sense of connectedness increases, then our compassion increases. As our sense of compassion increases then our sense of connectedness increases. The Dalai Lama would suggest that every single human being that you come into contact with has relevance to your life and you in turn are relevant to their lives. Our present moment connectedness will demand a response. Within this interconnectedness, the response is one of compassion, this really matters. And as informed Christians, seeking to be faithful disciples, then compassion can, and hopefully will be, that response. Compassion is thinking something, then saying, or doing something which has the aim of improving the situation or the well-being of somebody else. But being compassionate involves risk, love in action involves risk, and that risk can involve suffering hurt, rejection and sacrifice.

By virtue of the incredible advances in technology and communications, it is possible to be in contact with very many more people than our grandparents were. I am sure you can think of the various different ways that you connect to people electronically, as well as in person. But the question is to which level do you connect to these people? I suspect it might be with very much less depth than our grandparents. The call, in various places in the New Testament, is to be fully aware of our interconnectedness, our mutual dependence on one another as parts of the same body, with the recognition that 'I am because we are'. Mindfulness can assist us with that awareness, with that attitude of being connected, with that seeking to be mutually compassionate. There is no point in one part of the body saying to another – I have no need of you. This is incorrect. I do need you. And you need me despite our differences, despite our different approaches, despite our different backgrounds. The loving kindness mindfulness meditation encourages an awareness of that mutual need.

Possibility: with one person that you meet in person today, engage in conversation and see if it is possible to be a little more connected or discover a new thing you have in common? You may be pleasantly surprised!

I Am

Then Jesus declared, "I am the bread of life. Whoever comes to me will never go hungry, and whoever believes in me will never be thirsty."
John 6 v 33

God said to Moses, 'I am who I am. This is what you are to say to the Israelites: I am has sent you.'
Exodus 3 v 14

The only person you are destined to become, is the person you decide to be.
Ralph Waldo Emerson

Life is too deep for words, sit down to try to describe it, just live it.
CS Lewis

'I think therefore I am' wrote Rene Descartes (1596–1650). I wonder how his brilliant intellect would cope with today? And here are some alternatives to his famous quote:

I log on, therefore I am.
I am on my Facebook page, therefore I am.
I am, what I think you think I am.

I really like the short poem 'I am' by Helen Mallicoat. I have read it out in various settings, including church services. In a few short lines, she reminds us of what God is like:

When you live in the past,
With its mistakes and regrets,

It is hard. I am not there.
*My name is not **I was.***

When you live in the future,
With its problems and fears,
It is hard. I am not there.
*My name is not **I will be.***

When you live in this moment
It is not hard. I am here.
*My name is **I am.***

God is the I am. When God appears to Moses, (Exodus 3 v 14), it was not 'I was the creator' nor 'I will be present sometime later'. No, God appears and says, 'I am.' God is saying to Moses: I am with you, now I invite you to be with me now, in this present moment.

Jesus makes various claims about himself, declaring Himself to be 'I am...'. In John's Gospel, the writer captures seven 'I am' sayings from Jesus. One of these sayings is that Jesus says 'I am the Bread of Life' (John 6 v 33–35). This phrase is said with great symbolism. It recalls the story of the Israelites wandering in the wilderness, of their reliance on manna for food. It recalls that this manna was made available one day at a time, for today, for now. The manna was not for yesterday or for tomorrow (except on the Sabbath). Manna was a reminder to live in the present.

In John chapter 8, the phrase I am appears five times. I am... means that for Jesus he is expressing that He is fully God and fully human and that He is fully present. Jesus is not just saying wonderful words, but He is also expressing his experience – the Christian life is experiential. For us, the Christian life, the mindful life, is experiential: I am walking, I am breathing, I am meditating... We can add our own other words to this sequence. At this very moment: I am reading. And these words describe our experiences of being and living, in the present moment.

John the Baptist knows who he is. He knows that he is a voice crying in the wilderness. But John also knows what he is not. He knows he is not the Christ; he knows that he is not the Messiah. It is very good to know who we are and who we are not! When I am using text or WhatsApp on my phone, and try to sign off with a 'David', the predictive text often seeks to add Beckham or Cameron. I am neither one of these talented people. I am not the David who fought Goliath in the Old Testament. I am an ordinary David, with good points and bad points. But in the eyes of God, I am unique and special.

Similarly, it is good for you to know who you are. I am………………………………………………… fill in your own details! And having filled in your name, you can know that 'I am'. And the 'I am' that you are, is a person with good points and bad points. But you also are able to say 'I am unique and special'.

Whereas John the Baptist seems to be clear about who he is and who he is not, Peter the disciple gets into a muddle and into great difficulties at times. Near to the end of the gospel story, Peter is asked three times whether he is a follower of Christ? Before the cock crows, he answers three times 'I am not'. It is both interesting, and complex; what might be going on here? What we do know, however, is that Peter is not in the present moment. He is in the future, fearful of the consequences of saying 'yes, I am a follower of Jesus'. He is also in the past, remembering what fate has befallen other followers of Jesus. So, we can all learn from this. Fear, anxiety, lack of truth occurs when we are in the past (I was) or the future (I will be) instead of in the present (I am). The song by Chris Bowater 'Here I Am' emphasises being wholly available to Christ. Not partly available, not partly somewhere else. Here I am wholly available, nowhere else to be, nothing to achieve, here I am present with You.

Possibility: consider telling someone about the Zulu exchange of greetings Sawubona [I see you. I bring you into existence] and reply Ngikhona [I am here]. Reflect on using these words.

Jesus

Live like Jesus did, and the world will listen.
Mahatma Gandhi

With Jesus as the centre of your life, you will never be disappointed.
Pope Francis

I trust that you don't find this section is too contrived. What I believe, and, what I'm seeking to show in this section, is that Jesus permeates all aspects of mindfulness. At the same time, for me, mindfulness helps me focus on and understand Jesus better. My sincere hope is that this will become more true for you as well. I am going to cross reference to many of the other sections of this book.

The attitude of Jesus was that He should do the will of God (the Creator, Source, Father, Mother):

'If it is possible for this Cup to pass from me, but not My will but Thy will be done.' Even the most difficult aspects of the ministry of Jesus were done with the right attitude. Jesus was awake and alert, even in the Garden of Gethsemane when the disciples go to sleep. We see in the gospels He is awake to the needs of those around Him.

Jesus comes to earth, born as a baby and living on earth in the form of a body. And in that body, he suffers pain and the distractions of temptations just as we do. In that body, Jesus breathes. And very near the end, he breathes the Holy Spirit into the disciples. Jesus invites the disciples and those around Him to make a change, to turn from a life of sin and selfishness to a new life centred around compassion. The parables and stories that he tells challenge people about what they are doing or not doing. In His teaching, he also challenges people to sometimes be, rather than do.

Jesus is fully human and fully divine and, of course, this is incredibly difficult for the disciples and the people of Israel to discern. Jesus challenges them to open their eyes, and by doing so, they might see who He is, and also who they are. They might also see how they are driven along by their own ego. Jesus offers forgiveness for wrong-doing, and freedom to do the right thing. He counters the need to be getting there, recognising how important it is to give time to others. At every step of the way, Jesus shows gratitude for food, for people, for miracles.

And as He teaches, particularly in the Sermon on the Mount, Jesus wants us to have happiness. One example of the type of happiness we might have is by having humility, as Jesus himself has humility. John's Gospel structures the life of Jesus around the seven 'I am' sayings. 'I am' being an important part of mindfulness – rather than I was or I will be. And in making these claims, Jesus connects to each and every one of us (e.g., living water for the woman at the well), at the same time clearly identifying it we are interconnected, particularly in the way that we treat one another.

At the time of judgement, it will be our treatment of each other that really matters. To what degree we showed kindness to one another. And whether we did this at the right time, the *Kairos* time, that Jesus talked about so many times in the gospel. Jesus synthesised the whole of his message into just two commandments which were about love: love of God and love of our neighbour.

At intervals in the gospel story we read that Jesus detaches himself for prayer and meditation, preparing Himself for difficult times. He recognised the mind can get busy with distractions, with being in other times instead of the now. Being in the now requires non striving, because the mind will often wish things were otherwise or better. Jesus encourages us to have an open mind about how we might be different, encouraging Martha to note how Mary behaves. He suggests to Martha how she might have more oneness with Himself, and with her own self. And as she does this, she might have the added benefits of peace in her own heart and also patience with her sister. Jesus may well have spoken to Martha about how a time of quiet helps with living this challenging and difficult life. And as they ate the meal she prepared, how relishing each mouthful makes the food taste so much better.

In his teaching, it is clear that Jesus is fully aware of our temptation to re-think and remember events and conversations that have happened. And just how much this rethinking can affect and diminish our sense of self. In times of silence, our thinking can work overtime, and we are tempted to fill in the silence with TV, phone, Internet – anything to make the unpleasant thoughts go away.

Time can go at different speeds, depending on our state of mind and how present or distracted we are by thoughts. It can become difficult to appreciate just how special and unique we are – each and every one of us. In this struggle, to appreciate that the benefits of mindfulness are universally available – to Christian, atheist, agnostic, to people of other faith groups – is wonderful. Our vulnerability and the voice of the inner critic in our heads might try to persuade us otherwise, leading us to ever greater worry, and even worrying about worry.

Jesus offers us the chance to wake up, like the prodigal son, whether we are extrovert or introvert, wake up to the chance to experience a new life in Him. You have the chance to do this. You have the chance to discover more about mindfulness. Like Zacchaeus who was given a fresh start by his encounter with Jesus, through mindfulness, you can have more of the zest and abundant life that Jesus wants you to have.

Possibility: the shortest verse in the Bible; 'Jesus wept'. Jesus showed humanity, sensitivity, love, He didn't say 'follow this theology', but 'follow me'. In all our moments, even when we weep, we can 'Follow Him'.

Judgement

Do not judge, and you will not be judged. Do not condemn, and you will not be condemned. Forgive, and you will be forgiven.
Luke 6 v 37

Jesus said, 'Stop judging by mere appearances, but instead judge correctly.'
John 7 v 24

Why do you look at the speck of sawdust in your brother's eye, and pay no attention to the plank in your own eye?
Matthew 7 v 3

It is a great wisdom to know how to be silent, and to look neither at the remarks, nor the deeds, nor the lives of others.
John of the Cross

Judging others makes us blind, whereas love is illuminating.
Dietrich Bonhoeffer

Sometimes our lives require that we exercise judgement. For example, I have been involved in interviewing large numbers of people in my working life (for jobs, promotions and students). This requires discernment and judgement. Some psychologists say decisions are made within the first 3 minutes of the interview, some even suggest that, decisions happen in the first 30 seconds. Perhaps in these cases less discernment and more prejudice is occurring? As the old saying goes 'do not judge by appearances', because, 'appearances can be deceptive'.

Judgement can happen quickly, and sometimes, can happen unintentionally. We make judgements on the basis of the exterior, and what we see in front of us, not realising, what lies behind the face, the clothing, and what is said. Susan David* in her book *Emotional Agility* (pp. 28–33) refers to this process as 'heuristics', sometimes referred to as 'rules of thumb'. Susan David suggests that these heuristics 'kick in the moment we meet someone and immediately determine whether we want to know her better or steer clear'. Theses judgements, rules of thumb, are made on the basis of very little information. On many occasions they may match up with the longer term and more informed view based on very much more information, but on other occasions these judgements are either stereotyping or simply wrong! The hard thing is to alter the initial view. Hidden behind the initial view is a whole life story. And the whole life story is known only to God.

Saint Therese,* a French Carmelite nun, recognised the central importance of not being judgemental. For Therese, this meant accepting, with patience, whatever presented itself to her. And this attitude of patience seems to be one of the keys. Judging ourselves can be so debilitating. Being judgemental is a bit like being trapped in chains. The habitual judging of other people and ourselves is quite a prison, but mindfulness can help free us. Mindfulness is not about suppressing judgemental thoughts. We are encouraged (2 Corinthians 10 v 5) to bring into captivity every judgemental thought. And by this, it means I think noticing and observing these judgemental thoughts. Mindfulness can also help us notice the difference between judgement and discernment.

Even when seeking to do a mindfulness practice, self-judgement can arise very quickly.

Judgements like 'the last time I did this breathing practice it was so much better' or 'well, I am never going to be as good as person X' and then even potentially escalating it up to 'will I ever get this mindfulness?' For many of us, including me, this kind of judgemental activity has been a lifetime habit. (If medals were awarded for self-judgement, then I am sure I would have been in contention!) What can we do in all this barrage of judgemental thoughts? Notice more, observe more, allow more. Mindfulness has helped many people (including me) to do this.

The verse Romans 12 v 2 can perhaps allow us to begin this road to freedom. When we judge things, or more particularly people, by whether we like them or not, we are immediately restricting them, constraining them and diminishing them. And then by restricting or constraining them, we are also doing the same to ourselves. Much of our judgemental nature is linked to self-esteem. Our level of self-esteem often requires that we compare ourselves with others, build ourselves up in comparison to others, and in this process, we change them and limit them to suit our own needs and values. When we consider the abundant life (zest) that Jesus wants us to have, this restricting and constraining seems very unhelpful. By being awake, by being fully present, we significantly increase our chances of reducing our judgemental nature.

When thinking about judgement, I think that a particularly good topic to consider is sport.

It really doesn't matter which standard of sport a person plays at; it is a world of judgements. Judgements about whether a ball is in or out, whether you believe you are able to beat the other player, whether the other player is honest with line calls, how they deliberately pick upon your weaker partner point after point, and, if there is an umpire, how competent they are. But in addition to the external judging, there is also internal judging and condemnation. Why did I miss that shot, oh there goes another one, my backhand is rubbish tonight, why don't I ever get better? If you add into the mix some tiredness, then things can get a whole lot worse a whole lot more quickly! In the past, I have been through all of these, and more. Mindfulness has helped me notice, and by noticing, allows me to smile at myself, which is very different to how I might have reacted previously.

When I did my eight-week course, we were encouraged by a teacher to bring along an object. The object was to be something from our lives, which demonstrated to us something about mindfulness. The object that I took along was a badminton feather shuttlecock. For me, badminton, and any racquet sport, provides an opportunity for a person to be mindful. Because once on the court, the focus of attention is on hitting the shuttle or the ball. Sure, there can be moments in between when judgement can kick in. But in the actual moments of playing, hitting the shuttle, thoughts about work, or childcare, or other problems, are relegated to the background, and lose their hold over you.

Possibility: at some point today, consider the amount of time that Jesus spent with judgemental people (scribes and pharisees) and those who were judged (sinners, tax gatherers), and what he said about judging others.

Kindness

Therefore, as God's chosen people, holy and dearly loved, clothe yourselves with compassion, kindness, humility, gentleness and patience.
Colossians 3 v 12–13

But the fruit of the Spirit is love, joy, peace, forbearance, kindness, goodness, faithfulness, gentleness and self-control. Against such things there is no law.
Galatians 5 v 22

Life's most persistent and urgent question is 'what are you doing for others?'
Martin Luther King Jr

All that you give to others, you are giving to yourself.
Anthony de Mello

Aristotle, the Greek philosopher, is quoted as saying 'educating the mind without educating the heart is no education at all'. Wordsworth argued that the best portion of life are unremembered nameless acts of kindness and love. Having worked in the University of Oxford for 31 years, among the best educators in the world, I wholeheartedly agree with Aristotle and Wordsworth. In the University I was greatly heartened to witness great acts of kindness by the students towards the homeless and the unloved of the city of Oxford. One of the abiding images of the coronavirus lockdown in the UK, was that of the 99-year-old former army veteran Captain Tom Moore walking round his garden 100 times before his one-hundredth birthday in order to raise funds for the NHS, to whom he was grateful, and, to whom he wished to reciprocate their kindness.

This fund-raising endeavour caught the imagination of the whole country. Captain Tom had set out to raise £1000. The total sum raised was over £30 million, which I am sure he could never have envisaged when he began walking round his garden.

Aesop suggested that 'no act of kindness, however small, is ever wasted. Kindness is more important than wisdom and this kindness is the beginning of wisdom.' Henry James is quoted as saying, 'Three things in human life are important. The first is to be kind. The second is to be kind. And the third is to be kind.' The smallest act of kindness, when carried out, is always more valuable than the greatest intention, which never comes to fruition. Emelia Earhart said, 'A single act of kindness throws out roots in all directions, and the roots spring up and make new trees.'

It might be helpful to consider kindness as being on a spectrum. And the spectrum might look something like this: noticing > awareness > discernment > kindness > compassion.

Noticing sounds quite an easy thing to do, and yet it needs practice because we are out of the habit of noticing. In mindfulness one of the things that people are encouraged to do is simply to notice. Once noticing starts to happen, awareness develops. This can take time, and again, requires practice. The noticing of our breath leads to greater awareness of how our breath is in any given moment, and how, for example, it is interacting with the rest of the body. And then as part of this awareness, discernment can happen. Our reaction to the discernment can go in a number of different directions, one of which is a potential for kindness. And out of this kindness can come real compassion. In the compassion section, I have written in some detail about the Good Samaritan. The Samaritan notices the person on the ground, is aware of the victim's situation, discerns what needs to be done, decides upon what acts of kindness are required, and shows real compassion to the victim. The Dalai Lama* said, 'My religion is very simple. My religion is kindness.' Whether the Samaritan was religious or not, we don't know. What we do know was that it was him, and not the other passers-by, including the priest, who stopped and carried out acts of kindness and compassion.

How we face our situations, the attitude that we have, really matters. An attitude of kindness to oneself and to others I have found always, always, to be beneficial. But it is not easy. With greater noticing, then greater awareness and discernment, then greater levels of kindness are possible.

Things can change when we allow self-kindness to be brought into the equation. We see many times in the gospel stories that Jesus is recorded as having compassion on others where he shows acts of kindness. It is a trait for us to imitate, to copy, to develop. But it does not come easily or without practice. As time goes on, I understand more and more, that self-kindness is not only a help for me, but also a help to those around me as well. Because when I, or you, are in a better place through self-kindness, then you and I are in a better place to show kindness to others.

In Mindfulness A Practical Guide to Finding Peace in a Frantic World course,* there is great emphasis on loving kindness. Track 7 on the CD is the called the befriending meditation. Part of the meditation aims to develop ease of being, freedom from suffering, and good health and happiness. The course recognises that some people find his hard, but nevertheless, encourages participants to do this so that they in turn can show true kindness and compassion to others. The Dalai Lama* says 'meditation and the pursuit of wisdom should always issue forth in acts of compassion for others'.

Possibility: say silently to yourself, perhaps 6 times: 'I aim to develop ease of being, freedom from suffering, and good health and happiness.' Allow a pause of a few moments between each time you repeat the phrase.

Kairos

Therefore, Jesus told them: 'My time is not yet here; for you any time will do.'
John 7 v 6

Be on guard! Be alert! You do not know when that time will come.
Mark 13 v 33

There is a time for everything, and a season for every activity under the heavens.
Ecclesiastes 3 v 1

Alice: 'How long is forever?' White Rabbit: 'Sometimes just one second.'
Lewis Carroll

Be happy in the moment, that's enough. Each moment is all we need, not more.
Mother Teresa

Elizabeth Belville (1854–1943) was known as the Greenwich Time Lady. She was a businesswoman from London, who followed on from her mother, Maria, and her father, John, in the business of 'selling time' to people. How this was achieved was by, each day, setting her accurate and expensive watch to the clock at Greenwich, which showed Greenwich Mean Time. She would the travel around London and 'sell' people the time, by letting them look at the watch and adjust theirs to match. Incredibly, this business lasted many years. What Elizabeth Belville was selling was Chronos time. Chronos time is measured by a chronometer, a watch, a clock. Chronological time is what we are used to in the UK. It is the perspective that most people use to govern their day. Chronos is the time on a watch, so, for example, it is 4.30 in the afternoon (or 16.30 on the 24 hours clock). The problem for many people is that Chronos time keeps relentlessly ticking along. We cannot slow it down; we cannot make it stop. Tick, tick, tick. Seconds pass by, minutes pass by and hours pass by. Time stops for no one, not for the rich or the poor.

Kairos time is quite different from Chronos time. To understand the distinction between *Kairos* time and Chronos time is quite important. *Kairos* and Chronos are two Greek words, which describe time in quite different ways! Chronos is quantitative, whereas *Kairos* is qualitative. *Kairos* is the right time, the opportune time, the moment when! We get the word *Kairos* from the person who was the youngest child of Zeus, the god of opportunity, and therefore *Kairos* is the critical or opportune moment. In a simple example, the Chronos time might be 10.45 on a Sunday morning. Fifteen chronological minutes after a service of worship has started. But it can also be the *Kairos* time, the time of worship, the time to pray and sing, and learn and give.

The slower day is not coming. The day which contains 30 or 36 hours is not coming. And so what many people do is postpone things until there is more time. Here is an example: I haven't got time to practise the piano each day, so I will postpone this until the weekend and do a longer session; I am too tired and have household chores to do at the weekend, so I will postpone until the holidays and do some intensive practice then; the holidays come and go and there is no opportunity; I can do the piano practice when I retire as I will have lots of time on my hands – apart from grandchildren, infirmity, lack of motivation etc. Postponing things, especially pleasurable things, until the weekend, the holidays or retirement or the empty nest is simply that – a postponement. Each postponement is the loss of pleasure, enjoyment or contentment now, today. Later may not happen for a number of reasons, or, may not happen in the way envisaged or hoped for. Illness or bereavement may get in the way. So we always lose out when we put essential things off. Martin Luther King said, 'The time is always right to do what is right.'

Jesus spoke of the *Kairos* time, by saying 'my time has not yet come'. The gospel is a series of Kairos events in the life of Jesus, and this should provide a model and an example for us. We have so many *Kairos* moments in our lives, so many opportunities, so many moments of serendipity, and every moment is a unique moment And, that unique moment will not come again. These *Kairos* moments are connected to everything that is around us, people, places, nature, living things, God. The unwise person says that they have no (Chronos) time to meditate. What they are really saying is, they have filled their Chronos time with all kinds of things – some of which may be essential such as childcare or work but some of which may be trivial choices such as TV programmes. The wise person has *Kairos* time to meditate because they seize the moment. Mindful meditation has less to do with Chronos time but more to do with quality of time, Kairos time. The quality of the time that we spend meditating is more important than the length of the time involved. Even if we spend 10 minutes meditating, this is 600 seconds which is a huge number of moments!

Attitude to time is critical and I really do mean critical. Mindfulness helps us to understand that there really is only one now. And after this one now, there is one more now, and then one more. Each moment unique and special, each moment now or never.

Possibility: listen/watch the John Mellencamp song (with lyrics) 'Your life is now' https://www.youtube.com/watch?v=0lRgWaY0HE4

Listening

Then Jesus said, 'Whoever has ears to hear, let them hear.'
Mark 4 v 9

The Lord came and stood there, calling as at other times,
'Samuel! Samuel!'
Then Samuel said, 'Speak, for your servant is listening.'
1 Samuel 3 v 10

God speaks in the silence of the heart. Listening is the
beginning of prayer.
Mother Teresa

The word 'listen' contains the same letters as the word 'silent'.
Alfred Brendel

Not only did Jesus listen to other people, in silence, He listened
to God. He went to desert places, solitary places and quiet places
to listen to God. Disappointingly for Jesus, his disciples in the
gospel story take a very long time to learn to listen to what is
going on, and to what it all means for themselves and for those
around him. Listening to God, and what God might have us do,
is about obedience. The word obedience comes from the Latin
ob-audire, which means to listen. I believe that this means we
also need to listen carefully to others, because in their words
maybe we will receive prompts as to how we might obediently
follow Jesus.

Conversation can sometimes be very competitive. I don't
mean just competing as to who has had the best holiday, or the
best experience, but also the actual mechanics of the conversation.
Sometimes there is a real art in being able to interject into a
conversation any contribution at all. And why? Because people are

so used to speaking about themselves, sometimes quite endlessly and boringly, and hardly drawing breath! And in group situations, there can be, of course, other people who are in the conversation on the edge of their seat, waiting for their opportunity to do exactly the same. While they are waiting, sometimes itching to get into the conversation, they are mentally and secretly practising and rehearsing what it is they want to say. At the same time, they are imagining how gripped the listeners are going to be with what they might have to say! Elsewhere in this book, I have mentioned just how difficult this might be for people who are more reflective, perhaps more introverted, in that they are more sensitive and caring about how they contribute to the conversation. And this waiting, and caring, is called attentive listening.

Attentive listening does require great sensitivity and great patience. And I think it also requires love and presence. The very best conversations I have experienced have involved a two-way process of speaking and listening. Good conversation requires words and silence, speaking and listening. Listening before answering. And actually, when involved in conversation, surely each person really does want to experience new things? Really good conversation provides an opportunity to learn, to be stimulated into new thought patterns and make new discoveries. All this can only come from attentive listening instead of endless speaking! The person who is willing to listen, ask and discover new things is exhibiting a beginner's mind in the art of conversation, which begins with learning about other people. And in due course may be learning about themselves as well.

In Mark's Gospel (Mark 7 v 31–37) we read about the wonderful healing of the man who suffered from deafness and a speech impediment of indistinct diction. Jesus opened the ears of the deaf man so that he could hear and opened his mouth so that he could speak clearly. This single act of healing is very much more than a physical healing by opening his ears, it is giving him a new and different life, where things change completely for him. This miracle of healing allows the deaf man to hear. But the gospel story also has instances when Jesus says to those around Him that they fail to hear, they fail to listen, and as a consequence they fail to follow.

Attentive listening to others is a skill which requires effort but is a skill that can be developed, learned and practised. One technique that I have used which is incredibly effective in a group situation involves the following: splitting into twos, chairs are arranged so that they are adjacent to one another but face the opposite directions. When there is a number of people in the room, participants are required to speak quietly. The person listening (B) inclines their ear closely so they can hear the speaker (A). The activity required that the first person (A) speaks for 3 minutes, and the second person (B) summarises in one minute what they have heard, followed by one minute when the speaker (A) has an opportunity to comment on the summary. Then the whole process is reversed, so that Person (A) becomes the listener. Both person A and person B are required to take turns, to listen attentively, and offer their summary with care and kindness to the other person. Many people who have done this, have afterwards commented how satisfying this process has been. Any participants in the room who suffer from impaired hearing and sometimes struggle with hearing in the larger setting, find that they have an opportunity to hear, and, be heard. Each time I have been involved in this turn taking and careful listening, I have found it satisfying and encouraging. I am sure that you feel the same, that when someone has taken time and care to attentively listen to what you have had to say, that you feel better. So, following the example set by Jesus, take opportunities when they arise to do this.

Possibility: with someone you trust, choose a defined topic, taking turns, carry out the technique described above. Reflect afterwards about the process.

Love

'A new command I give you: Love one another. As I have loved you, so you must love one another. By this everyone will know that you are my disciples, if you love one another.'
John 13 v 33–35

Dear friends, since God so loved us, we also ought to love one another. No one has ever seen God; but if we love one another, God lives in us and his love is made complete in us.
1 John 4 v 11–12

The first is this, 'Love the Lord your God with all your heart and with all your soul and with all your mind and with all your strength.' The second is this: 'Love your neighbour as yourself.' There is no commandment greater than these.
Mark 12 v 30 to 31

Our life is all grounded and rooted in love, and without love we may not live.
Julian of Norwich

Lord, grant that I might not so much seek to be loved, as to love.
Francis of Assisi

In the Jesus story, we can read in all four gospels that He has lots to say about love and compassion. The whole gospel story is really a story of love and compassion, not just spoken about, but thoroughly and completely worked out in His life. And so when Jesus is asked, what is the foremost commandment of all, he answers (Mark 12 v 30 to 31) with two instructions, two challenges, two life giving gifts: 'to love God with all that we have, and, to love our neighbour as ourselves'. And if you are ever challenged to describe your Christian faith to another person, this is a simple and succinct reply that you can give. If you want to reduce the story of God, Jesus and our lives, we can do this in just one word. Love. Gandhi echoes this when he says, 'Where there is love there is life.' This is not the superficial love of pop songs. This is true and deep and gritty love.

But we all need to enact love, rather than just speak about it or describe it. Love needs to be in the real world, moment by moment. And in the real world that is around us, it is filled with real people of different shapes and sizes, of different levels of intellect, who are pleasant and unpleasant personalities. The real world is filled with a complete range of people together with their characteristics. All this offers to us opportunities to love right now, right here, right where we are. This love for others, in the right here and right now, often involves suffering and pain and hardship. Mother Teresa said, 'People are unreasonable, illogical and self-centred, but love them anyway.' We have all met the kind of people that Mother Teresa is talking about! Maya Angelou wrote that 'love recognizes no barriers. It jumps hurdles, leaps fences, penetrates walls to arrive at its destination full of hope'.

The incredibly well-known parable of the Good Samaritan (Luke 10 v 36), provides much opportunity for learning. In the parable, the victim provides a potential for an act of kindness and love to those who pass by. Goethe suggests that 'we are shaped and fashioned by what we love'.

We too have scenarios that present themselves, in the present moment, which are also opportunities to which we can respond, learn and in particular show love to others. We can be shaped and fashioned. But those opportunities need to be taken in the present moment, because the situation will have changed tomorrow, or the next week. We have the opportunity to respond to the scenarios that present themselves to us. We have the opportunity to act in each and every scenario that we are in. The more we are present, the more we act as well as react.

Just for a moment, borrowing from Buddhism, the first thing that the Buddha did after his enlightenment was to go back and show love and compassion to those around him. This part of the Buddha's life story provides an example and model for Buddhists. But of course, it also provides a model for Christians. And the gospel is all about the same. What a challenge! What a range of possibilities! What a privilege! But this challenge, this range of possibilities can also bring forward anxiety and fear – about the scenarios and also about whether we have the capacity or ability required. Mindfulness can help us gain freedom from fear. Jesus exhorts us to have this freedom. In this freedom we have greater possibilities for love. Timothy Radcliffe in his wonderful recent book *Alive in God* (p. 36) quotes the Dominican Henry McCabe who said, 'If you love you will get hurt and possibly killed. If you do not love you are dead already.' By living in the present moment, we will gain greater awareness and self-compassion, a less judgemental and fearful attitude to others, and these attitudes together will enable us to show greater fearless love.

it is very interesting to note that when you go on an aeroplane and are given the health and safety instructions by the cabin staff that one of the instructions is this: when you are faced with having to put on the oxygen masks, you are required to put on yours first, and then, having done this securely, attend to others including children. The instruction almost seems selfish. It almost seems counter intuitive. But what the instructions are telling us is how much more useful and loving we can be to others, when we ourselves are safe and equipped. From the well of self-compassion and self-kindness can come forth, in many ways, many acts of love and kindness to others.

Possibility: sit quietly and bring to mind a person you love or have loved. Give thanks for having this person in your life.

Mind

Love the Lord your God with all your heart and with all your soul and with all your mind.
Matthew 22 v 37

The person with the spirit makes judgments about all things, but such a person is not subject to merely human judgments, for who has known the mind of the Lord, so as to instruct them? But we have the mind of Christ.
1 Corinthians 2 v 16

Do not conform to the pattern of this world, but be transformed by the renewing of your mind. Then you will be able to test and approve what God's will is—God's good, pleasing and perfect will.
Romans 12 v 2

To meet everything and everyone through stillness, instead of mental noise, is the greatest gift you can offer the universe.
Eckhart Tolle

Owning your story can be hard, but not nearly as difficult as spending our lives running from it.
Brene Brown

Both Augustine* and Thomas Aquinas* suggested that the higher part of the mind is communing with God. We are called (Matthew 22 v 37) to love God with all our heart, all our soul and all our mind. Our mind is involved! Our minds are important in determining how we are towards God and how we are towards ourselves. The mind is an incredible creation capable of amazing complexity and understanding. But when the mind is not required to calculate or compute, when it is invited to just contemplate, then the mind can get a bit lost. The mind can start to react to its lack of computational requirements – and it reacts by introducing calculations of its own. What does it busy itself with? Replaying past events, but not just re-playing them, but adding to them judgements and interpretations and prejudices. It also busies itself with pre-playing future events, which by definition includes a huge amount of fiction, because they haven't taken place yet! And because the mind is such a good calculator, it can add to the pre-playing of events anxiety, stress and worry.

In *Paradise Lost,* John Milton writes 'the mind is its own place, and in itself, can make a heaven of hell, and a hell of heaven'. The times when we are flourishing, we can experience joy and peace and a sense of purpose. At other times when we are not flourishing, we may be drawn to anaesthetics of different types: television, alcohol, shopping, to try to help us cope with the anxiety and the difficulty. The advertising industry, on behalf of vendors, does huge amounts to persuade us to eat and drink certain products, to wear certain clothes, drive types of cars etc., etc. They understand how to provide the anaesthetic that we sometimes crave.

The brain is amazingly neuroplastic. The parts which thrive and the parts which diminish, depend on usage. The mind muscles, synapses, depend on you and what you dwell on. There is much research highlighted in the *Sane New World* by Ruby Wax* about how meditation and a different attitude to life can bring about a *rewiring* of the brain, a strengthening of certain *brain muscles.* The law of gravity is no surprise to people when they see things fall to the ground. We learn about gravity at school at an early age and witness it happening all the time. The law of the mind is a surprise to people! And this law is that whatever our mind dwells upon affects the mind and how it works and how it is stimulated.

Learning to drive was a torment for me. I failed my driving test four times. I just never thought that I would get it! The anticipation would cause me sometimes to shake physically at the start of a driving test. At my lowest times, I thought I would never be able to drive. And yet now, decades later, with no accidents and many tens of thousands of miles driven, I wonder why? Why was my mind and body so uncoordinated? Why was my mind and body so nervous about the process of driving? Instead, now, my body and mind are so relaxed into this process. The 'mind muscles' have got totally in tune with the body and requirements of driving.

The humorous phrase is: 'Minds need to be like parachutes. Minds, like parachutes are better when they are open'! The mind can easily be influenced by what we hear from others. When taking a service, it is still expected that at the end of the service, I stand at the back by the exit and shake hands with the congregation members as they leave. The mind can get busy very quickly with the positive, and of course, the not so positive comments. It is interesting to note how my mind can influence mood and even behaviour. But I have learned, and continue to learn that this is just the ego and the mind working overtime – especially when realising and remembering that anything of value that arises in the service comes from God.

In this country, the rose is considered to be a plant of great beauty. In addition to the beauty of the petals, the aroma and the foliage, the rose also has sharp thorns. We may wish the thorns not to be there. We may get hurt by them. But the thorns form part of the life of the rose in the same way as colour and aroma. Thorns can also form part of our lives. We may wish the thorns not to be there but it is from the thorns, the hurts, that we can learn.

A common phrase that I have heard mindfulness teachers use when encouraging students is to have a 'beginner's mind'. I think that the term 'beginner's mind' comes from the Buddhist tradition. It is a very helpful one as it corresponds to the suggestion by Jesus that we should be like children. Children have an openness and curiosity. As they learn and discover things for the first time they are, in effect, beginners at what they are doing, seeing or experiencing.

Possibility: on your next walk, however short or near, have a 'beginner's mind' to something or some things that you encounter on the way – almost as if you are seeing the thing(s) for the very first time.

Meditation

Devote yourselves to prayer, being watchful and thankful.
Colossians 4 v 2

For now, we see only a reflection as in a mirror; then we shall see face to face. Now I know in part; then I shall know fully, even as I am fully known.
1 Corinthians 13 v 12

Meditation is the only intentional, systematic, human activity which is not about trying to improve yourself, or get anywhere else, but simply to realise where you already are.
Jon Kabat-Zinn

Meditation is not a means to an end. It is both the means, and, the end.
Jiddu Krishnamurti

Formal meditation practice times are when you are deliberately sitting, lying down (or even standing). You set aside time to simply be, to meditate. This can then provide a resource pool for when the messiness of life comes along in the rest of the day. The difficult times which may be stressful or cause anxiety. It is at these problematic times when we can dip our foot into the pool and draw upon this resource. If we are feeling particularly stressed, then dive right into the pool! Meditation has no point unless it is firmly rooted in the everyday messiness of life which is happening. Studies show that even after only 8 weeks of a 20 minutes a day meditation, changes happen to the brain. Other studies show that these changes in the brain have positive effects on memory, mood and attitude. It is not, however, that you are having this as an aim when you are doing the meditation. Rather, it is that these positive benefits might come along because of the mindful meditation.

Mindful meditation is not easy! There are many books written about how to meditate. Meditation is a bit like prayer in the sense that again, there are many books written, but it is still quite difficult to actually do! There will often be, and maybe always be, chatter in your head as to why you are not going to meditate today. The excuses that might come along might include any of the following: 'I'm too busy', 'I'm too stressed', 'I'm too tired', 'I'm not very good at this', 'it doesn't work, so what's the point!'

Sometimes I think of meditation a bit like dieting when you are overweight. When seeking to lose weight, there is the intention to diet, but you don't want to because of the foodstuffs that provide such a temptation, and attraction, and which get in the way. When you are seeking to lose weight, if you can envisage the whole picture of a healthy person rather than just the foodstuff in front of you on the plate, the situation and the attitude change. Similarly, with mindful meditation, when you are faced with temptations towards other habits, you can envisage the whole picture of a healthier person with much greater well-being, then things can be different. When people say that they cannot meditate it simply is not true. Every single person *can* meditate. When they say that they cannot meditate, what they are really saying is that they are not prepared to set aside time to allow the possibility. Instead they want one more look at the Internet, at the television, at a magazine. Like piano practice, lots of shorter periods of meditation are better than none at all. Don't let perfection get in the way of the good, perfection might be 30 minutes a day every day *but* never achieved. Good might be just managing 5 or 10 minutes most days. The good is better than the non-existent perfection.

Mindful meditation seems to help the brain in a number of ways. One of the ways it seems to help is by elongating the moment between the stimulus and the moment that we make a response. What we are talking about here are very, very short units of time, but the elongation can make a huge difference to the response that we make in any given situation.

The difference between saying or not saying, doing or not doing something that you later regret and remember.

Some people confuse mindful meditation with feeling calm or serene. During the time of meditation, it is very possible that you may not be calm. Indeed, you may be quite distracted or agitated. Mindfulness meditation is not about feeling a certain way such as calm, serene or happy. Rather, it is about noticing how the mind is in this present moment, and in this present moment, and then this present moment and so on until the end of the meditation. Breathing techniques can help greatly with being present and drawing the attention of the mind to the present moment. It is not especially a hard task to find a method of meditation to use, the difficulty lies instead in developing the right attitude. This attitude hopefully will be open and welcoming and joyful.

After the meditation it is all too easy to make a judgement about how well, or not, the meditation might have gone. The *feeling* might be that it had gone well or not gone well at all. Either of these feelings may not be a true reflection on how beneficial the meditation might have been.

Humility is required at all times, and with this humility, judgement subsides. We are all beginners and need a beginner's mind because there is so much to learn however experienced or inexperienced at meditation our ego might try to tell us that we are. Ultimately, mindfulness meditation is being yourself, being more of yourself and less the demands of how other people would have you be. Just being. Just being you.

Possibility: consider again the quote from Jon Kabat-Zinn above.

Non-striving

Therefore, I tell you, do not worry about your life, what you will eat or drink; or about your body, what you will wear. Is not life more than food, and the body more than clothes? Look at the birds of the air; they do not sow or reap or store away in barns, and yet God feeds them. Are you not much more valuable than they?
Matthew 6 v 25–26

But seek first his kingdom and his righteousness, and all these things will be given to you as well. Therefore do not worry about tomorrow, for tomorrow will worry about itself. Each day has enough trouble of its own.
Matthew 6 v 33–34

There are two ways to get enough. One is to accumulate more and more. The other is desire less.
GK Chesterton

If you do not know where you want to go, it doesn't matter which path you take.
Lewis Carroll

In all our activities of life there is a difference between 'making things happen' and 'letting things happen'. At the right time, both can be good. But I have noticed, too often, that seeking to make things happen, can be detrimental to letting things happen. When you read and hear the life stories of a significant number of writers, inventors, and world shapers, what is noticeable, is that they seem to have a knack of letting things happen as well as seeking to make things happen. Quite often, in their non-striving, spontaneous, letting things happen times creativity happens.

So, to be clear, non-striving is not a passive state. Non-striving is not sleepiness or laziness. Non-striving requires us to be alert and attentive to who we are and where we are. This non-striving happens in the same way that being present to God requires us to be alert and attentive. Non-striving is a term used by Buddhists. And because of this, unfortunately, is often thought by Christians to be a trait for Buddhists only, and therefore not something to be embraced. This is a great shame! I believe the non-striving is very much a trait for Christians as well. It is unfortunate to exclude any good thing from one's life because of an anxiety that it might be a tenet of another faith group. Kindness is common to many faith groups and something we would not wish to exclude from our lives.

John Kabat-Zinn* is a US clinician who seeks to help his patients with relief for pain and stress. He can be considered a 'founder' of current day popular mindfulness, in particular the development of the programme called Mindfulness Based Stress Reduction (MBSR). Kabat-Zinn says 'that there is a very big difference between non doing and doing nothing'. He goes on to suggest that moments of non-doing are the greatest gifts that a person can give oneself. And why? Because the huge benefit of non-doing, of non-striving, is that there is nothing to achieve and therefore no need to worry about whether it will be of use or not.

In virtually all of the many definitions of mindfulness that I have read and heard, there is a phrase or element of the definition which says 'not wishing it were any different'. And this really is a key thing to understand. Mindfulness really is about non striving, not wishing things were any different, not constantly chasing after ways and means to make it different, better, smarter, etc. This echoes very closely a number of verses of the Sermon on the Mount. Here, Jesus speaks about not being anxious, not striving to store up treasures, not worrying about earthly things. And in the sermon, He suggests that this comes down to a stark choice. And the choice is seeking God or striving after earthly treasures (Matthew 6 v 25).

As part of our non-striving, we also need to be aware of the temptation of striving towards some imagined state of mindful and spiritual perfection. By striving to be perfect, we are missing the point completely. I have seen this striving among church people. A classic example is Jonny Wilkinson, the rugby player. He was driven in his rugby career, but also his whole life, by a fear of failure to be perfect. So even after playing great matches, he felt an anti-climax. I so hope that perhaps this book will offer a possibility of doing things in a different way. Instead of seeking to appear perfect to other people, we can simply be 'human'. This is quite difficult to explain, but by this I mean that although we are human, with human failings, but truly and genuinely seeking to be faithful and spiritual followers of Jesus. Only Jesus, who is our example, is perfect. This can take away so much of our worry. The first big step in this process is noticing. Noticing that we are worried or indeed being worried about worrying! Being 'human' is so much more preferable than being a worrier!

The mindful attitude of 'not wishing it were any different' is another way of saying having more acceptance of things as they are, particularly acceptance of things that we really cannot change. And once we can gain discernment of the difference between the things we might be able to change/do something about and the things we need not strive to change or make different, then a new possibility arises. And the new possibility is that we have in our lives more joy.

Possibility: spend a few moments during the day considering 'that there is a very big difference between non doing and doing nothing'. And contemplate how this might make a difference going forward.

Now

"The time has come," he said. "The kingdom of God has come near. Repent and believe the good news!"
Mark 1 v 15

Jesus replied, 'Let it be so now; it is proper for us to do this to fulfil all righteousness.' Then John consented.
Matthew 3 v 15

Jesus declared, 'Go now, and leave your life of sin.'
John 8 v 11

Springtime is at hand. When will you ever bloom, if not here and now?
Angelus Silesius

You cannot go back and change the beginning, but you can start where you are, and change the ending.
CS Lewis

Now! Now is the final one-word sentence from exasperated parent to their child. The word said as the psychological battle reaches its peak, and the parent is determined that it happens immediately. In this context, 'now' means not in 10 minutes, not tomorrow, not next week. 'Now' means in this moment. In this scenario, now is not a pleasant word for either the parent or the child. In complete contrast to this scenario, for those involved in mindfulness, 'now' is a wonderful and beautiful word. Now is a word that we are constantly exploring and seeking to understand.

In any sport, concentration towards effective shots requires the mind to be present, now. It requires that the mind is not thinking about the current score, or the number of points required to win the match. Thoughts about the score are all distractions. And in these distractions, the mind is moved away from the now, from the present, towards the future. And with this movement away from the present, if the score is unfavourable, there can be anxiety, anticipation or tension. The source of all this is the mind not being in the now.

Attentively watching the ball is very different to just looking at the ball. Attentively watching the ball requires the person to be fully present, fully in the now. Attentive eyes and mind instruct the body, so that in consequence, the body becomes present and alert to where the next ball will be. As a result, the body is able to move into position in readiness for the next shot, and then, to play the shot in the present. If you watch a very good tennis player like Roger Federer, you can notice that for the majority of his shots, he is making lots of tiny adjusting steps so that when he comes to hit the ball, he is in the best position possible to make a good shot. From my own experience, being completely present results in a more instinctive, natural and better shot. The shots are not so effective when time is occupied thinking about the consequences, the opponent or the impact on the score.

But practising being present, being in the now, is not just for those who play sport. It is possible and desirable for every single person. And it is possible and desirable in every aspect of life to practise being present, being in the now. It is also possible to observe when this is not happening, when you are not present in the now. There is no need to be harsh with yourself when you discover this happening because it is really common to most people, most of the time! And if you manage to catch yourself somewhere else, it may also be possible to observe where that is. And even possibly what has drawn you to that other place and time. Dale Carnegie encouraged us to 'remember, that today is the tomorrow that you worried about, yesterday'.

Thich Nhat Hanh suggests the miracle is not to walk on the water, but, rather, to walk on the earth always in the present moment. When we read the gospel account of Peter successfully walking on the water, it is an incredible amazing event. Interestingly, Peter starts to sink when he starts to think in the future, to think about what might happen next. He moves away from the successful *now moment* of walking on the water toward an unsuccessful *what if* moment of the future. Emily Dickinson* wrote that 'forever is composed of nows'. What you are is what you have already done. But what you will be is what you choose to do now.

Jesus says to the disciples (Mark 1 v 15): 'The Kingdom of God is at hand, the Kingdom of God is now.' The Kingdom of God is now or never. God is present now, in this moment, and because we experience repetitive series of now moments, God is always with us. The Dominican mystic Meister Eckhart wrote that 'there is but one now', and so to take the full opportunity that this one now offers to each and every person, including you. This is echoed by CS Lewis, who says 'that God wants us to attend to two things: the now and eternity'. And, by this, Lewis meant that by attending to the now, we are at the same time, attending to eternity.

I have been asked on a number of occasions, but what if now, the present moment, is not a particularly good moment, the present place is not a particularly good place to be? What if, instead, 'now' is painful or hurtful or troublesome? Jesus in the gospel story intersects with many people who are in a difficult and painful place (e.g., the woman who has been haemorrhaging for 12 years, the man full of a host of demons). Jesus intersects with them in these very messy and difficult times. Jesus intersects with us in our very messy or difficult times. Jesus meets people where they are, He talks, He listens, and He heals.

Possibility: do some mindful washing up! Allow yourself freedom from radio/TV, enjoy touch (bubbles in the water), smell, seeing the items as they are. Give yourself time to breathe and the opportunity to notice any tension in your body.

Open (Mary and Martha)

As Jesus and his disciples were are on their way, He came to a village where a woman named Martha opened her home to Him. She had a sister called Mary, who sat at the Lord's feet, listening to what He said. But Martha was distracted by all the preparations that had to be made. She came to him, and asked, 'Lord, do you not care that my sister has left me to do all the work by myself? Tell her to help me.' 'Martha, Martha,' the Lord answered, 'You are worried and upset about many things, but few things are needed, or indeed only one. Mary has chosen what is better, and it will not be taken away from her.'
Luke 10 v 38–42

Obeying God is listening to God, having an open heart, to follow the path of God points to us.
Pope Francis

There are no uninteresting things, only uninterested people.
GK Chesterton

Augustine teaches about the difference between the contemplative life and the active life. He goes on to suggest that there are three types of life, the contemplative life; the active life; and the life that combines both the contemplative and active. It may not be a binary choice of either/or, instead, it might be a choice of both. To have the choice of both we need to remain open to possibilities rather than have a closed mind in situations.

The story of Mary and Martha in Luke's Gospel appears to be a clear example of the contrast between the attentive listener Mary and an active person, Martha. Martha often gets a 'bad press', because she is the busy one. But actually, it needs to be remembered that Martha is holy and good, as well as being busy. However, in Luke's account, Jesus identifies that it is Mary who has the greater part, because it is Mary who has been the attentive listener. This passage could easily be set in this current year. There are so many 'Marthas'. In every church that I have been in, there has been at least one. In some churches they say 'thank goodness, we really could not do without her'. And it usually is a her, rather than a him.

In the Methodist church (which I am a member of), we have church stewards who are appointed for a small number of years (in my church 4 years). But there are many examples of stewards who have served for many more years and, sometimes have served as a steward for decades! Stewards on a plane are paid to give service to the needs of the passengers. A small number of busy people paid to service the numerous passengers passively sitting on the plane. Methodist Church stewards are not paid, but may sometimes be very much busier servicing the needs of the congregation who are passively sitting in the pews or chairs. The stewards, and the 'Marthas' in churches, are often exhausted. In their exhaustion, feeling that they cannot stop or let go. A question might arise as to whether these 'Marthas' get their self-worth, or, a distorted sense of self, by having to achieve all these activities. This obsession to be busy and valued seems contrary to my understanding with what Jesus encourages us to do both in this passage and in other places in the gospel. There is a lack of openness to another possibility of living, of being. An openness to mindfulness will help the balance between being and doing.

What we see in this passage is that the closed mind of Martha leads to resentment towards her younger sister, Mary. It is reminiscent of the resentment that the older brother has in the parable of the prodigal son. Both Martha and the older brother have an attitude problem. Both have the misguided notion that by 'working like slaves', they should be recognised, valued and rewarded. In this Mary and Martha story, Jesus has a different view. Jesus says that Mary has 'chosen the better part', recognising that she has made the choice to live in the present moment, to be available, to be present to Jesus and to listen attentively.

Jesus is not saying that simply listening is always better than preparing a meal. The meals in the gospel story are a critical part of understanding who Jesus is. Meals include the feeding of the 5000 and the last supper. What Jesus might be saying, however, is that sometimes, sometimes, we are required to open to being quiet, still and listening rather than being completely taken up with practical matters which can distract us and continually occupy us. It should not be forgotten, however, that Martha has also chosen to live in the present moment. She is the one who has opened her house, she is the one who has prepared food at the right time, she is the one who has attended to physical needs as well as the spiritual needs.

Surely Augustine is right, in that we need to be open and have an element of both in our lives, especially if we are driven, busy, active people. Rowan Williams* in his recent book *Luminaries: Twenty Lives That Illuminate the Christian Way* suggests (p. 68) that 'the condition we grow towards is one in which contemplation and action are inseparable. Being Christian is one thing: being present in the world with God at the centre of all your experience and from that hidden centre goes forward acts and words of your life'. He goes on to say that then 'there is no longer a gap between Mary and Martha'.

Possibility: is there an opportunity today to make a very small change in the balance of your doing and being, a little more space?

Oneness

Anyone who welcomes you welcomes me, and anyone who welcomes me, welcomes the one who sent me.
Matthew 10 v 40

Then Jesus cried out, 'Whoever believes in me does not believe in me only, but in the one who sent me.'
John 12 v 44

Remain in me, as I also remain in you. No branch can bear fruit by itself; it must remain in the vine. Neither can you bear fruit unless you remain in me.
John 15 v 4

Our task must be to free ourselves, by widening our circle of compassion, to embrace all living creatures and the whole of nature and its beauty.
Albert Einstein

Trust God that you are exactly who you are meant to be.
Teresa of Ávila

There is a song by KT Tunstall* which suggests that we are connected by little pieces of red thread.

At a concert I attended, she explained that this notion had come to her when seeing people moving around in an airport. Whether we know those around us or not, there is an interdependence. These imaginary threads pull us this way and that, we pull the same threads this way and that.

Coupled with this notion of threads holding us together, is the concept that we are just 'six degrees of separation' away from everyone in the world. This concept began with the

Hungarian author Frigyes Karinthy,* and has been developed by many people since. He suggests that by 'six handshakes', six communications in person or by post or email, we can reach anyone in the world. This concept might work because the, say 500, people we know, know a further 500 (although there will of course be some overlap), who in turn know, say, another 500 others. It potentially makes the world a very small world. It can be tested out by striking up conversations with strangers and soon discovering that somehow historically or currently, you have someone in common, even maybe in a different country.

I believe that mindfulness is universal, available to all. And this is because what we have in common with one another is far, far greater than what we have as differences. Mindfulness is available to all people, to people of all faith groups, and those who belong to no faith or religious grouping. Over the last few years, I participated and helped organise a mindfulness drop-in group. In the group have been Christians of various types and denominations, including Anglicans, Catholics and Methodists, but also people from a Jewish faith background. The group also made welcome agnostics and atheists. We can be one. It is possible!

Once a month the drop-in group has been participatory, where people share their ideas with one another. It is a time when we all can learn, and all can understand and appreciate the perspectives and insights that others have gained. The group sits in a circle and in the centre of the room and the group is a candle. The candle brings light into the room. Each and every person can see this light. Each and every person has that light available to them. It is the same light, seen from different angles depending on where the person is physically sitting in the room, but nevertheless available to one and all. The candle gives off life light to one and all, and by doing so is shortened; there is a cost to the candle. There can be a cost to our giving, as we choose to light the path for others.

The concept of one-ness can be explored at a much deeper

level. Julian of Norwich,* a Christian mystic from the 1300s, believed that through her 'one-ing' with God, she was equal and united with all humankind – all one soul, one human. Her description of 'one-ing' with God was like breathing in the love and awareness of God, so that, the essence of God is inhaled, imbued and imparted. And by breathing in, we can become awareness and love. And in this awareness, love can become interconnected and one with others. Being present, being aware, allows us to increase our sense and experience of being.

Eckhart Tolle*also explores this one-ness in his writings. He writes that underneath the surface appearance, everything is not only connected with everything else, but also with the source of all life out of which it came. Each person, each sentient being is connected to the source of all life. Each person, each sentient being is connected and at one. Getting in the way of this connection, getting in the way of this one-ness is our ego. Our ego wants more, wants to be important, wants to be recognised, wants to compare and to be superior. Our ego is not happy with true and deep humility, is not happy with true and deep one-ness.

Being at one with what is, the present moment, does not mean that you are incapacitated, that you are not able to plan ahead or move forward. In the present moment, in the what is, we can plan and decide what comes next. We can do this from a current moment awareness. We can do this from present moment humility. We can do this without the ego taking control of the situation and demanding more and better. Having one-ness with the present moment gives us one-ness with life. We become our lives, the abundant lives that Jesus so much wants us to have.

Possibility: when in a coffee shop, sitting waiting, spend some time people watching. Not particularly what clothes they are wearing, more their demeanour and their attitude. Reflect on how connected you are to everyone around you.

Peace

Peace I leave with you; My peace I give you. I do not give to you as the world gives. Do not let your hearts be troubled and do not be afraid.
John 14 v 27

Blessed are the peacemakers, for they will be called children of God.
Matthew 5 v 9

Let the peace of Christ rule in your hearts, since as members of one body you were called to peace. And be thankful.
Colossians 3 v 15

We can never obtain peace in the outer world, until we make peace with ourselves.
Dalai Lama

If you yourself are at peace, then there is at least some peace in the world.
Thomas Merton

It is good to ask ourselves from time to time what we understand by the word or concept of peace? Often people will define peace as an absence of something else. At a national level, peace might be described as an absence of war. On a personal level it might be described as an absence of stress and anxiety. Peace is not so much about the absence of trouble, but the relaxation of heart and mind in the midst of trouble. Peace is not freedom from the storms of life, but freedom in the middle of the storms. But it goes much deeper than that. And if it is much deeper than that, how do we go about promoting peace in our lives? The peace that is an offer from God, is a peace which transcends all human understanding. It is a peace which is dependable and lasting.

And how might mindfulness complement the peace that is an offer from Jesus (John 14 v 27), which is quoted above. RT Kendall* writes that 'inner peace is better than prestige, better than position, and better than pride'. Deep inner peace comes from not having to strive towards being some kind of super-Christian person, some kind of super-human that we're not meant to be. Once we are able to recalibrate what constitutes 'success', we can allow our lives to become simpler, more pleasurable and most of all, more peaceful. The peace on offer from Jesus is different from what the world is able to offer.

The Dalai Lama* is quoted as saying that 'world peace begins with inner peace'. This kind of peace is the result of retraining your mind to process life as it is, rather than as you think it should be. Eckhart Tolle,* is quoted as saying 'you find peace not by rearranging the circumstances of your life, but by realising who you are at the deepest level'. My sense is that this peace is encouraged and enhanced when we are able to be give more compassion to ourselves, and, more compassion to those around us. This self-compassion and compassion to all sentient beings around us, can in turn bring wholeness and the abundant life (zest) that Jesus promises to us all. But even in this abundant life, is a life full of ups and downs, good and bad times, troubled and happy times, times we feel at peace and times when we do not. The Buddhists say 'if you want peace, then be peace'. Being peace is a prerequisite for making peace. Being peace and making peace are contrary to the ego's natural instincts and activities.

Peacemakers are different from peace lovers. Most of us would say that we are peace lovers.

Peace lovers might list as important pleasures like: living in the countryside, liking the quiet life, watching slow moving TV. But peace making is very different. It is hard work, both in families and communities or nations. We only need to think of the truth and reconciliation committee in South Africa to know how difficult and demanding peacemaking is. We live in an era where peacemakers are in great demand in numerous situations. In the UK we still have the differences that were created between 'remainers' and 'brexiteers', between Conservative and Labour, and have a political system which encourages confrontation rather than cooperation.

In our efforts to obtain peace in our lives, our natural instinct is to seek to push away thoughts and circumstances which are not pleasant, and conversely to hang onto those thoughts and circumstances which are pleasant. In her best-selling book *Emotional Agility*, Susan David* explores this in detail by describing these tendencies as 'bottling' and 'brooding'. She explains that the suppression of these thoughts and emotions is just temporary and what happens is that they return. We seek the short-term gain of having what seems like peace. But, unfortunately, it is a pot of false gold. The unpleasant thoughts and emotions do indeed return, sometimes more forcefully than the first time. And as a consequence, peace disappears. We can never have peace of mind unless we have peace of heart. Without peace of, mind we can never have peace of body. What disturbs the peace of our body disturbs our peace of mind.

Sadness and depression can affect our bodies, with lethargy and pain. Mindfulness can help us notice when we are doing things. It can also help us notice when we are not doing these things which bring about lasting peace. The peace on offer through mindfulness is caring about hearts, minds and bodies, mental and physical well-being and through developing healthy and positive attitudes and habits.

Possibility: spend a whole day seeking to notice if there are people around you who appear to exude and encourage peace. And at the end of this day, reflect on this.

Patience

But if we hope for what we do not yet have, we wait for it patiently.
Romans 8 v 25

Be completely humble and gentle; be patient, bearing with one another in love.
Ephesians 4 v 2

Be patient, then, brothers and sisters, until the Lord's coming. See how the farmer waits for the land to yield its valuable crop, patiently waiting for the autumn and spring rains. You too, be patient and stand firm, because the Lord's coming is near.
James 5 v 7–8

Patience is the companion of wisdom.
Saint Augustine

To lose patience, is to lose the battle.
Mahatma Gandhi

I have read in several places the Henri Nouwen* illustration about the trapeze artists in the German circus Simoneit Barum. What Nouwen discovers when talking to the trapeze artists is that it is only one of the two artists who does the catching. She or he is the catcher. The other trapeze artist flying through the air must do nothing or suffer the consequences! The catcher does the catching. The flyer does the flying. The flyer must with patience, stillness and trust wait to be caught by the catcher. I cannot imagine what this feels like. But it must seem like an eternity flying in space, flying in a high risk and dangerous situation until caught by the catcher. In our lives, we are the flyer, and God is the catcher. With great patience, stillness and trust, in each and every moment, trust that God is always there to catch us.

Patience is listed as one of the fruits of the spirit (Galatians 5 v 22–23). Other fruits listed in these verses include topics covered in this book Love, Peace, Joy, Kindness. My own experience is that mindfulness can increase levels of patience, particularly in the area of conversation and attentive listening. You might say that attentive listening is not important, that there are far more important matters to give attention to. The next time you are out and about having conversations with people, notice how many times people are very prepared to talk about themselves and are not so keen to hear about you. Some people almost spend time waiting for their opportunity to add more detail about themselves, almost at your expense.

Whilst writing this book I had a kidney stone, which caused incredible pain. In fact, the pain was unlike anything I have ever experienced. In the following week or two after this experience, I mentioned in casual conversation what had happened. But before I could provide any detail, the mere mention of a kidney stone caused some people to give me huge amounts of detail about relatives who had kidney stones or gallstones. It really was a lesson in learning patience. (And the second lesson, to not choose such a topic again to open a conversation with!)

In Luke's Gospel (Luke 18 v 1–8), there is a parable about patience and persistence. As we seek to follow a spiritual life it requires great patience and persistence. As we seek to follow a mindful life it requires great patience and persistence. As we seek to do this, we do well to remember that God's timing is not our timing, and all too often our timing is not God's timing. Psalm 90 talks about a thousand years with God being like a day. The Israelites found it difficult to patiently wait upon God when in the desert. Forty years is a very long time when wandering, waiting and wondering. Sometimes it might seem that we are in a metaphorical desert where we too are wandering, waiting and wondering. Wondering if things might be different or better? Waiting for things to improve? Wandering from shop to shop, or job to job, or church to church. Nelson Mandela provides a fantastic example of patiently waiting. He does this for 27 years in a cell. Let us all be patient.

There are many things in life that take time. It takes time for fruit to ripen, it takes time for flowers to blossom, it takes time to become fluent in another language. The spiritual life takes time to mature and develop. The mindful life takes time to mature and develop. And all require that we are patient. Christian mindfulness can bring about great patience – waiting on God, waiting on the revealing of God, waiting on becoming more present to God, and waiting for the evidence of things not seen (Hebrews 11 v 1). Meditation practice and a mindful way of life need to be patiently cultivated. Part of that cultivation is a patient motivation to faithfully, and regularly, want to live the mindful and meditative life.

And as we seek to do this, we need to remember that we are not really seeking to get anywhere. It is not like a 1500-metres race where you are trying to get over the finishing line. This is not how the mindful life works. It is not a question of trying to reach the finishing line quickly. It is a matter of patience. There is no point in saying that by some superhuman effort you have a target within 12 months to live the completely mindful or completely patient or completely spiritual life. Quite the opposite, there is no target. Once you start, it is something that evolves over the rest of your life!

Possibility: Nelson Mandela was patient for 27 years, and changed the world! Consider being patient about something even for 27 hours. What might be different?

Questions

Thomas said to him, 'Lord, we don't know where you are going, so how can we know the way?'
John 14 v 5

Jesus replied, 'I will ask you one question. Answer me, and I will tell you by what authority I am doing these things.'
Mark 11 v 29

Learn from yesterday, live for today, hope for tomorrow. The important thing is not to stop questioning.
Albert Einstein

Judge a man by his questions, rather than his answers.
[Judge a person by their questions, rather than their answers.]
Voltaire

What is wisdom? Is it thinking that you have all the right answers? Or, is wisdom associated with having all the right questions? In John's Gospel, the disciple Thomas asks some of the key questions and arrives at great and wonderful truths for himself – and for us. It is possible to reach a distant goal by taking small steps. However, the key is to keep taking them. To reach the distant goal of abundant life, happiness and joy, then keep taking small steps. Steps of anticipation. Steps of open mindedness. And like Einstein suggests (above), as we make our small steps forward, not to stop asking questions along the way.

In this section there are some questions and there are some answers. I am not saying that they are all the questions that you might think are relevant and important. I am not saying that these are the right answers – this would be arrogant! But here are some questions that I hope might be useful, together with some answers that might lead you into further thinking. Included here are some questions that people have asked me...

Is mindful meditation and mindful living available to everyone?

Yes! Well, there is a simple and direct answer!

That is the wonderful thing about mindful meditation and mindful living, it is available to everyone. Please also look at the section 'Universal', which describes the all-party activities that have been happening in the Houses of Parliament. The report describes the various spheres of life that they believe mindfulness can help with, including in education and the workplace. With mindfulness, there is no certificate or diploma that we are seeking to achieve; instead, it is a lifetime learning opportunity, where having a beginner's mind throughout is helpful.

Is 'mindful meditation' and 'mindful living' an Eastern religion?

No! Many people associate mindfulness with Buddhism. It is true that mindfulness features in Buddhism. But it is not required that Buddhism features in mindfulness. I have found some teaching helpful, but never contradictory, to my own Christian faith. There is wisdom in other religions as well as in Christianity. There are common threads shared between the religions of kindness, love, and how we treat our neighbour.

Am I required to empty my mind?

No! I have heard this quite often as a fear or worry. Over several years, not once have I been asked to empty my mind, by either a teacher or a book. There is never any requirement to empty the mind. Rather, there is an invitation to notice what is happening in the mind. Please turn to the sections about thoughts and re-thinking for a fuller explanation of this.

Is mindfulness only for young people?

No! There is no age barrier to mindfulness. It is available to everyone. Young and old. There are programmes in schools for young children. There is much research into teenage years and mindfulness, because for those who suffer from depression, often the first episodes happen in mid-teens. My experience has been that people of all ages have benefitted. On the courses I have been involved with, and, at the retreats I have attended, there have been people in their 70s and 80s. What is important is not chronological age, but having a beginner's mind, being open to the possibilities.

Does mindful meditation require me to sit in yoga positions on the floor?

No! During the mindful meditation, people adopt a pose that is comfortable for them. Most people sit on a chair. Some people, including those with back problems, elect to lie down.

Some people, because they find them more comfortable, use a kneeling stool (I find them really uncomfortable for my knees). Yoga positions are not required. Some people do elect on occasions to sit in a yoga position, but this is by personal preference.

Is Mindfulness just for the difficult times in my life?

My own introduction to mindfulness was by a counsellor in the University of Oxford. She was informing staff like me that it was a technique available for students going through very difficult times. But at the end of her talk, she made it clear that it is a helpful way of life for everyone who wanted greater well-being in their lives. So yes, it can help greatly in the difficult times. But yes, it can also help greatly at all times to encourage greater well-being for everyone.

Will I have time?

I can't answer this definitively for everyone. Especially for a parent of young children, especially for the carer looking after very dependent elderly relatives. Or for the worker with very long hours. This question occurs regularly. However busy, however stretched, whatever the demands on our lives, it has something to do with choices. One person who was very committed but found her workplace to be incredibly demanding found that her only place during the day for a three-minute breathing space practice was when she went to the toilet! It is possible to learn mindfulness in the supermarket checkout queue, changing nappies, on the train to work. So in that sense, each person can and will have time.

Possibility: spend a few moments jotting down your own questions.

Quiet

Rather, it should be that of your inner self, the unfading beauty of a gentle and quiet spirit, which is of great worth in God's sight.
1 Peter 3 v 4

He got up, rebuked the wind and said to the waves, 'Quiet! Be still!' Then the wind died down and it was completely calm.
Mark 4 v 39

...and to make it your ambition to lead a quiet life.
1 Thessalonians 4 v 11

If we do not have quiet in our minds, outward comfort will do now no more for us than a golden slipper on a gouty foot.
John Bunyan

Quiet people have the loudest minds.
Stephen Hawking

To make sense of the notes of a piece of music, it requires that there is silence between the notes. Taking this one step further, Debussy is quoted as saying that 'music is the silence between the notes'. The sound of the notes and the sound of the silence in between, completely complement one another to create the whole. Similarly, to make sense of the words, it requires that there is silence between the words. The words and the quiet have the potential to complement one another. To make real sense, attentive sense, of someone else's words, requires quiet.

When someone is distressed or anxious and wants to talk, often what they want is not lots of advice and instruction, rather they want quiet into which they can speak, into which they can be heard, into which they are able to explore. Good conversation is not waiting for the opportunity to tell the other person all about yourself, but also in creating quiet into which you are able to pay attention to the other person. This requires patience, this requires good listening, this requires sensitivity leading to empathy and perhaps sympathy. Ultimately, this requires love. The skill of providing sufficient quiet is a skill that can be learned and developed.

Most faith groups, and, many secular professionals involved in health and well-being, recognise and extol the benefits of quiet and stillness. Blaise Pascal* said, 'All of humanity's problems stem from man's [a person's] inability to sit quietly in a room.' To hear what God wants to say to us requires quiet and stillness. So frequently, there will be many intruding, competing and very tempting noises. Some of these noises will be external – including, for example, the temptation to be distracted by TV or music. Some of these noises will be internal: you must do more, you must do better.

In her helpful book *Quiet* by the academic Susan Cain,* she identifies that quiet, sensitive and reflective people are increasingly being regarded as second class citizens. At the same time, people who are risk-taking, insensitive and extrovert are being given more attention and acclaim. In her studies and observations, she identifies that what often happens in group situations is that the people who speak up first are considered to be more intelligent. But these people speak up first not because they are more intelligent (often the opposite), but because they are less reflective and less sensitive. In contrast, quiet and sensitive people will often reflect before they speak and so in some situations may not be heard much or at all. From personal experience, I can say that it can be incredibly frustrating not to be heard and, at the same time, to be considered less intelligent. We need diversity, we need inclusivity, we need variety. But most of all, we need to learn from one another. To do this we need those who are noisy, extrovert and insensitive to become more aware of those who are quiet introvert and sensitive.

If it was easy to quieten the mind, then we would all do it. However desirable, however much we are persuaded of the health benefits, it is not easy! It is actually really difficult! Here is a challenge for you. For five minutes, just stop reading this book, and try to be quiet and to stop thinking. Just for five minutes. If you manage for 50 seconds, it is quite an achievement. For some people even five seconds is quite hard! This kind of quiet comes with practice, this kind of transformation takes time, it takes a lifetime. Moving towards quiet and stillness requires for all of us a transformation of the habits and practices that we have taken a lifetime to perfect. And as we seek to make it a goal to live in a quieter way, then the distractions and temptations become more subtle and sophisticated.

In church, we 'hear' the story of when Elijah (1 Kings 19 v 1–17) is waiting on the mountain for God. In the story, God is not in the wind, the earthquake or the fire. God is in stillness, in the quiet, in the silence. Elijah hears God's still, small voice. Here is a challenge for all of us. For us to hear that still, quiet, small voice then we ourselves need to be quiet, because living in our own noise we have little chance. We need to be mindful. For us to be quiet requires us to be present. For us to be quiet requires that I am not lost in the disagreement with my employer yesterday, the anxiety of meeting my extended family for an event tomorrow, the overbearing person at church on Sunday. These are all impediments to the quiet and still mind.

Possibility: hearing happens without effort, but it is us, our ego, our thoughts that get in the way. Spend a few moments in quiet, allowing the sounds around you to be heard. They are there all along.

Relishing (mindful eating)

...but don't let him know you are there until he has finished eating and drinking.
Ruth 3 v 3

I have compassion for these people; they have already been with me three days and have nothing to eat.
Mark 8 v 2

What one relishes, nourishes.
Benjamin Franklin

Mindful eating turns a simple meal into a spiritual experience.
Thich Nhat Hanh

Around Christmas each year, the top 10 non-fiction book chart is filled with books about food, cooking, recipes, and then soon after Christmas, the book chart has lots of books about weight loss. Some years ago, there was on television, a programme with a very catchy title *You Are What You Eat*. The formulaic programme would have the presenter go to somebody's house, open the fridge door, and always demonstrate the same results: a fridge full of processed food instead of fresh fruit, salad or vegetables. There are so many books, magazines, YouTube channels telling you what to eat. With increasing numbers of people either overweight or obese, what you eat is really important. There is no judgement in *this* book, rather, great sympathy with those who are overweight but who would like to be different. Many people who are suffering this way realise that they need to do things differently – by eating less or differently combined with exercising more. But maybe there is another thing to consider!

Perhaps, it is not just about *what* you eat, but more about *how* you eat.

When we are in the present moment, we are more able to relish the food that we are eating. When we are in the present moment, we are more able to make decisions about whether we are hungry or just being tempted to eat something. Many people believe that they are eating according to how hungry they are. The reality, however, is that they are eating because of what is available. What is in the cupboard or the fridge greatly influences the choices that we make. The packaging and the advertising by food manufacturers goes a long way to influencing those choices. It is possible for us to mindfully plan ahead as to what we might eat in any given day. We can plan to have just three meals without snacking in between. With mindful eating, instead of the aim of seeking to lose weight, the aim would be to enjoy eating the food more slowly and attentively. By doing this, a by-product might be that you lose weight. But even if you don't lose weight, you still feel the benefits. But whether you are the right weight or overweight, it is possible to gain from mindful eating.

Just for a moment, I would like you to consider eating an orange. Ideally, you could actually do this in practice having read this section of the book. The first stage might be to express some gratitude for the recognition for the journey of the orange to your hand. Consider the grower, and all the care and attention that went into the growing of the orange, think about the food picker, the packer, those involved in the transportation to the UK, the shopworker involved in putting it out on the shelves, and even the bus driver if you travel by public transport enabling you to bring the orange home. And then in gratitude begin the process of eating the orange. The first stage might be to lift the orange, to feel its texture, to notice the indentations on the skin and the colour of the skin. And then to relish and savour the smell of the orange. Then, to spend time peeling the skin of the orange, and while doing so, employ as many sensations as possible, even listen carefully to the peeling process. Before actually putting the first piece in your mouth, again savour the smell and the texture of the individual piece. And then having the piece in your mouth, take time to notice the juices, the roughage, the size before actually biting and eventually swallowing. This whole process may take some time, but you may find the orange tastes significantly better. As an introduction to mindfulness in church services, I have invited people to do this with a raisin. Comments afterwards have included that 'this is the best raisin I have ever tasted!'. It is being about how to eat rather than what to eat. It has been about relishing and savouring the item of food.

In contrast, mindless eating is when we are tempted to eat without really appreciating what it is we are eating. Instead of savouring one raisin, it might be grabbing a little handful and consuming them quickly. Instead of paying attention to the food, it might be paying attention to the television, doing a puzzle, glancing at a mobile phone or maybe all three things at the same time as trying to eat!

Eating well involves all of the senses. Our eyes to appreciate the colour and form of the food, our nose to smell the aroma, our touch to get a sense of the texture, our ears to hear any sounds and then our mind to fully appreciate gratefully what we have in front of us. In the Lord's Prayer we say 'give us our daily bread'. This is a reminder to appreciate each and every day our 'daily bread'. For the Israelites this was daily manna. Our manna may be from the supermarket, the street market or the food bank. It may be oranges. Whatever the food and whatever the source, I encourage you to mindfully relish and savour each moment of eating.

Possibility: choose an item of food, like an orange, and follow the steps outlined above.

Re-thinking (and Remembering)

Do you have eyes but fail to see, and ears but fail to hear?
And don't you remember?
Mark 8 v 18

I thank my God every time I remember you.
Philippians 1 v 3

Can any one of you by worrying add a single hour to your life?
Matthew 6 v 27

Don't live in the past, don't ponder about the future, stay in the present moment, now, always.
Mark Twain

To the quiet mind, all things are possible.
Meister Eckhart

In the creation story of us, as people, as humans, we have as part of that creation, been given minds. And our minds think. Thinking can be wonderful, imaginative and beautiful. Thinking about and contemplation about God is good. Thinking about beauty is amazing. Thinking about love is good. Thinking about how to show compassion and kindness is good. Our thoughts lead to choices and in turn our choices can lead to actions. These actions can soon become habits and then the sum of our habits is our lifestyle. Good thoughts, good thinking can have a profound effect on our lifestyle in a very beneficial and life affirming way.

I once heard the following humorous description of pleasant and unpleasant thoughts. The talk was given by Chris Cullen (see Universal). He mentioned that pleasant thoughts are like Teflon, non-stick, not hanging around, going as quickly as they came. In contrast, he then described unpleasant thoughts to be much more like Velcro, hanging around, sticky, not wishing to leave. Isn't it amazing that, for so many of us, this is true? And yet, when a pleasant thought comes along our natural inclination is to try really hard to hold onto that thought. Conversely, when an unpleasant thought comes along our natural inclination is to try and push it away as soon as possible. Despite all our efforts, both holding on and pushing away, Chris Cullen's analogy still holds true – in that the Velcro thoughts do stick around, giving us the opportunity, unfortunately to re-think the thoughts, to bring back and remember associated previous thoughts.

Eckhart Tolle* suggests that thinking can make you suffer more than anything else. Often it is not the thinking about the situation that makes us suffer, but the thinking about the thinking of the situation that really leads to suffering. As we do this re-thinking, as we start to add interpretation and nuancing to what might have actually happened in the first place, the situation deteriorates. Sometimes there is nothing heavier than a thought. It is almost as if the thought is like a dead weight. It becomes heavy and difficult to bear. If only it was a rucksack which perhaps you can put down or leave in the left luggage store. No, this heavy weight is borne on the inside, seemingly inside your very body.

We are very much more than our thoughts. I believe this strongly. Psychologists believe this. Buddhists believe this. Christians need to believe this! This is a vital truth to grasp hold of. This is because thoughts can trap, ensnare and imprison us. If you, or someone that you know, suffers from depression or anxiety, then you will be aware that this imprisonment creates a spiral of looking inwards. A spiral of re-thinking and re-thinking. The thinking becomes a prison which stifles the possibility of abundant life (zest).

The thought producing entity inside us, the mind, is a powerful entity. It is an entity with lots and lots of practice! The practice for all of us has developed over the years into ingrained and persistent habits (which is why we find it difficult to have a beginner's mind, a childlike enquiring mind). There is a wonderful liberation possible when we come to the realisation that our thoughts are not facts and therefore, that we are not our thoughts. An even greater liberation is possible when we come to the realisation that the commentary is just that, a commentary. Likewise, this commentary is not fact. This liberation, this wonderful release is available to Christians, to atheists, to Buddhists, to people of any faith and none.

As we, ourselves, are more than our thoughts, in the same way other people around us are more than our thoughts of them. Our thoughts about them can, and will, limit them. And we can use these thoughts to judge them, to pigeonhole them, and to have prejudice against them.

In addition to re-thinking, we can also easily get caught in our memories, our remembering – somehow hoping these memories are transformed into something different, where we become someone different. It is possible for us to lose time and energy in this process. And why? Because with our memories there is a temptation to hold onto the pleasant ones and to push away the unpleasant ones. But our memories make up our lifetime journey, our emotional journey and our spiritual journey. Bad memories can bind, chain and constrain us. But when we live in the present, and observe them just as memories, the power of these bad memories diminishes. Our memories of the past can be full of regret and become quite distorted versions of what actually happened. This can ruin our present life.

Through a mindful approach, when the memories, the thoughts that you have been re-thinking have been particularly scathing, then it is possible to say thank you to these views and then, having acknowledged them for just what they are, allow movement forward. Our present life can recognise memories for what they are, and we can become free.

Possibility: on a number of occasions today (perhaps 6), when troublesome thoughts arise say to yourself 'I am not my thoughts, I have thoughts'.

Self

What good is it for someone to gain the whole world, and yet lose or forfeit their very self?
Luke 9 v 24–5

So I say, walk by the Spirit, and you will not gratify the desires of the flesh.
Galatians 5 v 16

You were taught, with regard to your former way of life, to put off your old self, which is being corrupted by its deceitful desires; to be made new in the attitude of your minds; and to put on the new self, created to be like God in true righteousness and holiness.
Ephesians 4 v 22–4

What makes us human is not our mind, but our heart, not our ability to think, but our ability to love.
Henri Nouwen

The more deeply we are our true selves, the less self is in us.
Meister Eckhart

So many people derive their self-worth from what others think of them. So many people aspire to be someone else, a different version of themselves. To have different qualities: witty, slim, intelligent, popular etc. Many years ago, I worked with a highly gifted individual. He went on to become a professor, but at the time that I knew him he was one step away from being a professor. He was a clinician and academic, someone who was also gifted at music having been awarded a music scholarship to the University of Oxford. And yet despite all his skills and abilities, he suffered greatly from self-doubt. He compared himself with the one person in the field who had achieved just a little bit more. And by comparing himself with this person, undermined his very self. Curiously 99% of the population would envy his talents, his achievements and his wealth. The struggle that he put himself through was because of this comparison.

No one can see right inside us. Our inner life and outer life are different. The skin protects all that is on the inside. If everyone could see right inside everyone, the world would be a very different place. All relationships would be different. Intentions and desires would be different. It is almost impossible to imagine what this kind of world might be like. Mindfulness is present moment awareness. And in this present moment awareness, the spirit leads us to present moment possibilities. As this happens, we become more aware of our self. Not the exterior self that we present to others, but our own deep, real self. Some people might also call this our very soul. One of the difficult things that is required of us in our life of discipleship is to try to increasingly create some kind of alignment between my 'self' and Jesus. Alignment between the 'I am' of myself and the 'I am' of Jesus. Jesus is not theological, not just a good idea, but a person. And it is with the person of Jesus that we seek everyday alignment and every moment alignment.

Augustine wrote about the problems of self-hood, self-knowledge and self-awareness. He expresses surprise about just how much time and effort an individual can spend noticing other things, without first noticing their own self. He argues that the necessary condition for knowing oneself is that we must come to ourselves, stop wandering and start the journey to selfhood.

Eleanor Roosevelt wrote, 'Remember always that you not only have the right to be an individual, you have an obligation to be one.' She achieved great things, both in the US as 'first lady', and at the United Nations, where she helped to author the UN Universal Declaration of Human Rights. Article one states

'All human beings are born free and equal in dignity and rights.' Being your self matters! You are always with your own 'self', so you might as well enjoy the company!

I have mentioned that one of the most significant things that I have discovered through mindfulness is self-compassion, with the emphasis on the word self. Too many sermons, too much exposure to fundamental, conservative, legalistic Christianity has created bad habits. And for those, like me, who have tendencies towards perfectionism, self-compassion becomes even harder to achieve. But what I have discovered, and I now very firmly believe is that it is difficult to have compassion towards other people without first having compassion to yourself and that it is difficult to love other people without first loving yourself. Our interconnectedness with other beings, with other people who also have a unique self, depends on mutual love – love for other selves and love for your own self. This compassion for self and other selves can be learned. Compassion can be practised so that it becomes more habitual. And this compassion towards your own self can have a huge and transforming impact on a life. It can bring increased levels of well-being and more joy.

In the story of the Good Samaritan, we see the that the Samaritan, the type and race of person considered by many Jews to be inferior, shows great compassion toward a stranger, someone from another race, someone from whom he could not expect to gain a reward. We are not told in the story what happens to his very self. My suspicion is that the Samaritan went home feeling just a bit better, just a bit more joyful, just a bit more connected to his self. As readers, we can only speculate whether he told anyone else what he had done. It may be that he was like Jesus encouraged us to be, someone who gave this assistance and compassion secretly, a person who gave 'with one hand without the other hand knowing' (Matthew 6 v 3–4).

When we are down, anxious or depressed we get a smaller sense of our self. We get a narrower view of our self, and we can become self-absorbed and self-pitying. Self-pity can be addictive. Self-pity is destructive. The verse Romans 12 v 3 can be a help to get things into perspective. It can allow us to get a right and compassionate opinion of ourselves. And this might allow us to have a more mindful, wider self-view, a view which is more open, creative, appreciative and one which leads to a self which has more possibilities, more energy and greater enjoyment.

Possibility: spend a few moments to recall one matter where you may not be showing much self-compassion to yourself. Having identified this, spend a little time showing kindness and compassion to yourself about this one matter.

Silence

Very early in the morning, while it was still dark, Jesus got up, left the house and went to a solitary place where he prayed. Simon and his companions went to look for him, and when they found him, they exclaimed, 'Everyone is looking for you.' Jesus replied, 'Let us go somewhere else, to the nearby villages, so I can preach there also. That is why I have come.'
Mark 1 v 35–38

But Jesus often withdrew to lonely places and prayed.
Luke 5 v 16

In silence, God ceases to be an object, and becomes an experience.
Thomas Merton

This silence, this moment, every moment. If it's genuinely inside you, brings what you need.
Rumi

I really like the story of the student who approaches a teacher to explain wisdom. The story begins with the student going to see the teacher, with just one thing on their mind – and that is to understand more about wisdom. The student asks a series of questions. When the teacher hears the questions, the teacher remains silent. So, the student asks the teacher the same questions a couple more times, but again the teacher remains silent. The student is frustrated. The teacher notices this frustration. Then after another period of silence, the teacher says to the student, 'I am teaching you now, but you are not listening.'

Sadly, even silence has class distinctions. The disadvantaged often need to tolerate more noise in the workplace, more noise in their homes (because they are more closely packed together), more noise in their cars because they are older, more noise in the neighbourhood because there are more people. All of these things together have a huge impact on their well-being, and consequently, their longevity. Silence therefore becomes a luxury item. If only people could understand this then silence would become more valuable than jewellery or top of the range cars. Silence, for many people, has become more desperately sought after than ever in the twenty-first century.

Jesus often withdraws to lonely places (Luke 5 v 16). No iPad, no phone, no YouTube videos. Instead, silence. It appears that in the silence growth happens, readiness develops and love expands. It would be so fascinating to know exactly what happened for Jesus during these times? How much chatter did He have inside His own head? How many times did He withdraw? And for how long? Some of these times of withdrawal coincide with key moments in the gospel story – for example, as He is about to choose the 12 disciples, the night before his crucifixion...

Jesus (and Buddha) both withdraw to silent locations so that they can better understand life and how to live it. Jesus spends time alone (Mark 1 v 35–38). He is in silence. He is in stillness. It is here that He can prepare. It is here that He can make Himself ready. The disciples have not come with Him. Their track record is not great! If we think about their time in the Garden of Gethsemane near to the end when they fall asleep. They haven't yet understood, haven't made progress in their spiritual lives, haven't discerned yet the importance of the time of silence and stillness and preparation for the busy times, the demanding times, the times when great energy is required.

Silence is not just absence of sound. Silence is much deeper than this. Beyond the immediate silence is a greater silence in which we can experience the eternal. In silence, God can be heard. It is interesting that the Genesis story relates how God spoke into the silence. And then to read in Revelation (Revelation

8 v 1), that at the opening of the seventh seal, there was silence in heaven for half an hour. (I am sorry that, like many parts of Revelation, I have no idea what this means!) God can speak into *our* silence as well. My experience at church services is that there is insufficient room or time for silence. Over recent times, I have introduced more silence to the services that I lead, in prayers, in reflection time on the readings and in preparation time. As people leave the services, there are positive comments about this. There is a desire I believe for more silence. In the silence, there are no differences of opinion, no disputes about theology, no clashes of personality with others at church. Thoughts can of course interrupt the silence. But the silence itself is precious.

On one of the mindfulness courses that I helped with, two of the participants suffered from tinnitus. It was interesting and incredibly informative when they shared about this 'near madness' that arose for them from this lack of silence. It made me reflect upon those who do not suffer from tinnitus. Often in our own seeking to be silent, we can notice self-made noise. Songs (sometimes the most annoying and catchy ones!) are heard which go around and around in our heads, thoughts and anxieties that arise spin around, voices from years ago re-emerge and berate us. Mindfulness helps us make choices which allow us to switch off these distractions and noises. By being present, by noticing, you will gradually find it easier to turn away from these noises and distractions.

'If you love truth, be a lover of silence,' said Thomas Merton.* The deepest human experiences often require silence. In deep silence, much can be heard, discerned and discovered. It is in the silence that God can speak to us and prompt us. It is in the silence that we can listen more attentively to the love of God as it seeks to permeate us and cause us to love. Coming to silence can take time, but it is time well spent.

Possibility: spend a few moments considering the notes on a page of music. The edges of the notes come into contact with and are surrounded by the white space of the page, which remains silent. The notes when played are surrounded by silence.

Thoughts

We demolish arguments and every pretension that sets itself up against the knowledge of God, and we take captive every thought to make it obedient to Christ.

2 Corinthians 10 v 5

Remain in me, as I also remain in you. No branch can bear fruit by itself; it must remain in the vine. Neither can you bear fruit unless you remain in me.

John 15 v 4

You do not think your way into a new kind of living. You live your way into a new kind of thinking.

Henri Nouwen

Thoughts in your head are really no different to the sound of the bird outside. It is just that you decide that they are more, or less, relevant.

Adyashanti

Much of our time is spent thinking. Estimates vary how many thoughts we have each day, but range between 50,000 to 80,000! That is a huge number of thoughts! I do wonder how this can be calculated? For what type of person? We are so very different. Sometimes it is possible to catch ourselves having a quickfire succession of thoughts. I am very conscious of this sometimes when I have gone upstairs to fetch something, but on arrival have forgotten what, because in the meantime I have had a stream of other thoughts in my mind. At other times of the day, the sequence of thoughts seems to pass by almost unnoticed.

The imagery used in the Mindfulness A Practical Guide to Finding Peace in a Frantic World course*is that thoughts are like clouds in the sky. The clouds might be light and wispy, equating perhaps to light and happy thoughts, passing by quickly and effortlessly. But there might also be thoughts like dark, heavy clouds, lingering oppressively. But each type and size of cloud are simply clouds. And however long they stay, for whatever shape they are, the (hopefully blue) sky remains behind the clouds.

Mindfulness does not mean changing your thinking or suppressing your thinking. Nor is it about seeking to replace thoughts with more positive thoughts or more pleasant thoughts. Mindfulness is much more about observing your thoughts, noticing your thoughts, and beginning to discern the patterns and habitual thinking that you might have. And once you have noticed, to learn to let them go. Jesus is very aware that our minds can get caught up with repetitive thinking, introspective thinking and negative thinking. Jesus calls us (Mark 1 v 15) to have a radical change of mind about our whole way of life, a change from a worldly life to a life of discipleship.

Paul addresses this matter in his letter to the Romans. We are encouraged (Romans 12 v 2) towards a change in our pattern of thinking, to be transformed by the renewing of our mind. What a wonderful encouragement.

Teresa of Ávila* wrote that thoughts are like unquiet little gnats in the night. If you have ever tried to get to sleep in a room where there is a fly or a mosquito buzzing about, then you will remember just how distracting the 'unquiet little gnats' are. However, it can make a difference if you believe that the buzzing noise might be harmful to you. So if you think that it might be a wasp or a bee you might think differently than if it is just a buzzy fly. Teresa of Ávila also commented that the harder you try not to think of anything the more aroused your mind will become and you think even more. So many people can identify with this, especially in the early hours of the morning. This can escalate very quickly, so that in addition to the original thoughts, a commentary can get added to the thoughts.

In a slightly different situation, if you are with others and the distracting noise is something that you are responsible for, then you might think differently about the situation than if you had no responsibility. The noise can seem louder and more insistent when you have in addition the weight of expectation of others to deal with the issue. Having responsibility somehow adds to the urgency of the situation. I used to feel this acutely when in my job I was responsible for a fire alarm system covering many buildings including residential blocks. There was huge expectation for me to sort this out quickly and efficiently. Thoughts would sometimes race, because the ego became very active! But on one occasion when I went to a mindfulness drop-in, without having any responsibility, then a fire alarm fault in the building was something to learn from, rather than to have to anxiously deal with. The thoughts were completely different.

Thoughts are not facts, they are events. Like any event, large or small, we can observe the event. We can observe what type of thought that we're having. We can observe how many times the thoughts return or, morph into a similar thought. And, once we can get into the habit of observing our thoughts, we can increase our chances of not being overwhelmed and absorbed by these thoughts. We might even on occasions be able to go one step further, by being able to name the thought, e.g., 'I name this thought anger or worry'. If we are able, with humility and patience, to observe and notice and listen to our thoughts, then this can help us immensely. We are then no longer our thoughts, but an observer, a person noticing, a person listening. In this patient and humble observation and listening we have more chance of allowing thoughts to come and go rather than dominating and overpowering us.

Possibility: when you next have a chance, buy a bottle of bubbles. And then from time to time, blow the bubbles high into the air, and consider thoughts like these bubbles. [Imagine this until you are able to get a bottle.]

Time

See, I have told you ahead of time.
Matthew 24 v 25

"The time has come," he said. "The kingdom of God has come near. Repent and believe the good news!"
Mark 1 v 15

Therefore, Jesus told them, "My time is not yet here; for you any time will do."
John 7 v 6

We must not allow the clock and the calendar to blind us to the fact that each moment of life is a miracle and mystery.
HG Wells

All we have to decide, is what to do with the time that is given us.
JRR Tolkien

Clocks and watches are a recently modern construct. Hours and minutes are just artificial divisions of time. An hour might have been shorter or longer when first constructed. But hours and minutes are the construct which advanced society has put in place to determine how we divide each day. Yet, time can seem to go at different speeds. Quoted, in many places, is the observation made by Albert Einstein about time. He suggests that if you have your hand on a stove for just a few seconds, it can seem like an eternity, but in contrast, sit with a pretty girl (or handsome man) for an hour, and it can seem like a minute. Even when people are at the same activity, for example, a lunch gathering, time can go more quickly or slowly for different people at the lunch – depending on who they are sitting next to and how the conversation goes. If a person at the lunch party would really rather be somewhere else, then time can move slowly. If a person is engrossed in conversation, time passes quickly.

Occasionally when waiting at traffic lights, when the light has been red, my attention has been taken by something or someone inside or outside the car. However, in these situations, the moment that the lights change can bring out the worst of impatience in other people. Within a moment or two, literally a moment or two, people start beeping their horns. John Ortberg calls this the 'honkosecond' – one of the shortest measures of time known to humans! This is the time from the green light showing its colour to the time the impatient driver behind showing their true colours! Sometimes the air is blue with bad language!

Time is a diminishing resource. For, no matter who we are or how wealthy or talented a person might be, time is diminishing by 24 hours each and every day! We spend many of our resources on fast things. For example: fast broadband, instant credit and fast cars. This is because so much of society suggests to us that not being fast is to be a loser. The pressure is huge. And yet, despite all the time saving devices, much of our savings are evaporated into the next thing: looking at Facebook, watching YouTube, following tweets. Time saving devices, particularly those inside the kitchen and including laundry related should have been liberating. Sadly, time has been directed toward other activities, instead of finding peace or silence or rest.

Going on a retreat can be a wonderful experience. Going on a retreat completely alters you, especially if the retreat gives plenty of space for silence and non-doing. A good retreat, I think, is one where you are encouraged to switch off your phone, tablet or laptop. Some people find that they are so prone to temptation that the best thing for them is to actually hand the devices in. The silence and the stillness can alter the perception of time during a retreat. For some people, the arrival time is scary as they come to the realisation that all that normally determines their day, all that normally obligates them each day, the noisy stimuli on which they base their life is taken away. Time changes, or at least, the perception of time changes. In the Gospel of Mark, the word 'immediately' is often used (39 times in my version though less in the NIV) as the scenes transition from one to another. It is almost as if the gospel writer is in a hurry to explain the gospel story. And yet, Jesus seems to take his time (e.g., on his way to Lazarus, or when praying in the desert).

In sentences when people are speaking about time, the choice of verbs is quite varied. The phrase which I like least like, and never use, is 'killing time'. I find it quite sad that a person could regard time in such a way. At the other end of the scale, somebody might say 'I have really enjoyed my time here', or that 'time has really flown by'. Many times, I have heard the phrase 'if only I had more time'. Assuming a life span of just 70 years (projections in the United Kingdom are greater than this now), then this equates to 25,000 days. And assuming 16 waking hours each day, then this adds up to 400,000 hours! How much more time do people need?

As mentioned, clocks and watches are the instruments by which we measure time. However, the time itself is mysterious. Your watch might say 1.25.34 pm (thirty four seconds after twenty five past one in the afternoon). What you watch does not tell you, however, is that the time is this moment! And then one second later, the second hand on your watch may have moved on (1.25.35), but again it does not tell you the time is this present moment. The second moment (1.25.35) just described is the future of the first moment (1.25.34) just described. For each and every moment, you really cannot completely anticipate what will happen in the next moment. My encouragement to all readers is, as far as we are able, to mindfully live and enjoy each and every moment.

Possibility: for part (or all) of the day, take off your watch and notice (including any anxiety that might arise by not knowing the chronological time).

Unique

The Spirit testifies with our spirit that we are God's children.
Romans 8 v 16

If the whole body were an eye, where would the sense of hearing be? If the whole body were an ear, where would the sense of smell be? But in fact, God has placed the parts in the body, every one of them, just as God wanted them to be.
1 Corinthians 12 v 22–24

But you are a chosen people, a royal priesthood, a holy nation, God's special possession, that you may declare the praises of him who called you out of darkness into his wonderful light.
1 Peter 2 v 9

God loves each of us, as if there were only one of us.
Saint Augustine

In a world of prayer, we are all equal in the sense that each of us is a unique person, with a unique perspective on the world, a member of a class of one.
WH Auden

In services I sometimes use a humorous reading which is a spoof of an HR consultancy company making comments about and helping Jesus choose His disciples. The overall conclusion is:

'It is our opinion that most of your nominees are lacking in the background, education and aptitude for the type of enterprise you are undertaking. They do not have the team concept. We would recommend that you continue your search for persons of experience in managerial ability and proven capability.'

And then, some of the disciples are evaluated and their

particular qualities highlighted:

'Simon Peter is emotionally unstable and given to fits of temper. Andrew has absolutely no qualities of leadership. The two brothers, James and John, the sons of Zebedee, place personal interest above company loyalty. Thomas demonstrates a questioning attitude that would tend to undermine morale.'

The humorous ending to the spoof reading is:

'One of the candidates, however, shows great potential. He is a man of ability and resourcefulness, meets people well, has a keen business mind and has contacts in high places. He is highly motivated, ambitious and innovative.'

Well, of course you can guess who!

The reading is designed to provoke a reaction. And each time I hear it, my reaction is always the same. Thank goodness! Thank goodness that Jesus chose the very disciples that he did. Each one unique, each one special, each one, including Judas, someone that we can learn from. This gratitude even includes the disciples who are in the background, who seemingly do not have major plans to play in the unfolding of the gospel story. This is a very helpful model, especially people in quieter supportive roles who neither seek nor grab attention from others (1 Corinthians 12 v 22–24). Levi was called by Jesus to be one of his twelve disciples. An incredible choice by Jesus. A tax collector (bad enough!) representing an occupying force from hundreds of miles away – what could be much worse? And yet Jesus chose Levi. And as a result, Jesus Himself would receive unpleasant and abusive treatment from the pious people around because he did to mix with tax collectors (and sinners).

John Ortberg has written a book with the great title: *If You Want to Walk on the Water, You've Got to Get Out of the Boat*. Jeff Lucas has written a different book called *Staying in the Boat and Other Things I Wish I'd Known*. They both advocate what their respective titles suggest. I believe that both concepts are important to understand. And why? Because our unique set of skills, personality and calling that we have, may demand that we do something very dramatic like Peter, or, something undramatic like the remaining disciples as they stay in the boat.

Most people seek to define us by our age, our skin colour, our height or our job title. Some of these attributes we might share with others (e.g., being 5 foot 5 inches tall) or are roles that we have in common (e.g., working in a shop). But what really defines us and what makes each one of us unique, is what it is that we are really living for? And coupled with this, our uniqueness is also defined by what it is that is preventing us from living these things? This happens to us all. It is how we come to terms with this difference that is important. These are very big questions! Do please give yourself some time and space to consider these questions. Our answers, our attitude to these questions is what really defines us.

In the introduction to her book *I Thought There Would Be Cake*, Katharine Welby-Roberts (daughter of the Archbishop of Canterbury), identifies that she would like to start believing more that she is unique and valuable. Her self-doubts and lack of self-worth is explored in the book. She wants to reach a point where she understands more fully that she is unique, is worthy of love from God, from others and from herself. We are unique and special. Each one of us. You and me (Romans 8 v 16). How much time and emotional energy do we waste wishing it was somehow different, wishing we were somewhere different, wishing we were someone different?

Mindfulness helps us to come to terms with who we are. Mindfulness helps us to come to not wishing it was somehow different. Mindfulness helps us to not waste so much time and emotional energy trying to being someone different.

Possibility: consider someone you know well and what you find unique about them.

Universal

He [Peter] saw heaven opened and something like a large sheet being let down to earth by its four corners. Do not call anything impure that God has made clean.
Acts 10 v 11, 15

When they heard this, they had no further objections and praised God, saying, 'So then, even to Gentiles, God has granted repentance that leads to life.'
Acts 11 v 18

You are whole and also part of larger and larger circles of wholeness you may not even know about. You are never alone. And you already belong. You belong to humanity. You belong to life. You belong to this moment, this breath.
Jon Kabat-Zinn

If we practise mindfulness, we always have a place to be when we are afraid.
Thich Nhat Hanh

For this section, I have drawn heavily from the website called *The Mindfulness Initiative*. The information about this can be viewed on the House of Commons website.

https://www.themindfulnessinitiative.org/mindfulness-all-party-parliamentary-group

On this website there is a short video where Theresa May, the then Prime Minister, is asked in PMQs about her intentions to follow up the work of the all-party group. Her answer is a little waffley, but there is a humorous end to the clip, when John

Bercow makes an observation about the benefits of mindfulness to the Labour MP Chris Ruane, who asks the question.

The cross-party group compiled a report, which is available in physical form and as a pdf:

https://www.themindfulnessinitiative.org/Handlers/Download.
ashx?IDMF=1af56392-4cf1-4550-bdd1-72e809fa627a

The cross-party group identified in the report that it has a universal capacity:

> Mindfulness practices in various forms can be found in all the meditative wisdom traditions of humanity. In essence, mindfulness –being about attention, awareness, relationality, and caring – is a universal human capacity, akin to our capacity for language acquisition.

In the introduction to this impressive report, the cross-party group say:

> We have been impressed by the quality and range of evidence for the benefits of mindfulness and believe it has the potential to help many people to better health and flourishing. On a number of issues ranging from improving mental health and boosting productivity and creativity in the economy through to helping people with long-term conditions such as diabetes and obesity, mindfulness appears to have an impact.

They go on to suggest that more needs to be done:

> There is still much research to be done on how mindfulness training can be offered at scale in different settings and with different population groups, but what is already clear is that it is an important innovation in mental health which

warrants serious attention from politicians, policymakers, public services in health, education and criminal justice as well as employers, professional bodies, and the researchers, universities and donor foundations who can develop the evidence base further.

And the group makes these observations:

Mindfulness is one of the most promising prevention strategies and is regarded as popular and non-stigmatising, unlike some other mental health interventions. Mindfulness is a way of being in wise and purposeful relationship with one's experience, both inwardly and outwardly. It is cultivated by systematically exercising one's capacity for paying attention, on purpose, in the present moment, and non-judgementally, and by learning to inhabit and make use of the clarity, discernment, ethical understanding, and awareness that arise from tapping into one's own deep and innate interior resources for learning, growing, healing, and transformation, available to us across the lifespan by virtue of being human. It usually involves cultivating familiarity and intimacy with aspects of everyday experience that we often are unaware of, take for granted, or discount in terms of importance. These would include our experience of the present moment, our own bodies, our thoughts and emotions, and above all, our tacit and constraining assumptions and our highly conditioned habits of mind and behaviour. While the most systematic and comprehensive articulation of mindfulness and its related attributes stems from the Buddhist tradition, mindfulness is not a catechism, an ideology, a belief system, a technique or set of techniques, a religion, or a philosophy. It is best described as "a way of being".

Since 2013, cross-party groups from both the UK House of

Commons and House of Lords have attended the Mindfulness A Practical Guide to Finding Peace in a Frantic World course,* which I have mentioned in this book, and which was indeed the starting point for my own mindfulness journey. The website indicates that, as of April 2019, over 240 politicians have received training. The course was delivered by Professor Mark Williams and Chris Cullen who are from the Oxford Mindfulness Centre. Mark Williams is co-author of the book/course, and, it is his voice that you hear on the CD that accompanies the book, and forms part of the course.

The parliamentarians have also formed a weekly drop-in class that provides continued instruction, and for them fosters a community of practice, and I am sure (from personal experience) mutual support and encouragement. Some of the politicians found this particularly helpful, as they operate in an environment which is often adversarial and critical. The initiative has expanded its horizons to link up with other politicians and legislators around the world to encourage the benefits of mindfulness in their countries in various contexts of politics, administration and organisation.

In early 2014, The Mindfulness Initiative supported parliamentarians to set up a Mindfulness All-Party Parliamentary Group (MAPPG), with co-chairs from various political parties. The group has investigated why and how mindfulness might be helpful and beneficial in the following spheres:

Quoting directly from the website:

Education Can mindfulness in schools influence classroom behaviour, attention and focus, help raise educational standards, and develop young people's tools for well-being?
Healthcare Can mindfulness reduce the incidence of mental health problems such as depression, as well as help tackle long-term health conditions and improve public health?
Work Can mindfulness be a way to reduce stress and anxiety

– and develop resilience, emotional intelligence and creativity – in the workplace?

Criminal Justice Can mindfulness be a way to tackle depression, anxiety, stress in the criminal justice system?

Teaching standards There is currently no formal accreditation process for mindfulness teachers. As interest in training grows, how can people be pointed towards good mindfulness teachers?

Mindfulness really is a universal possibility, potentially available to everyone, whatever age, background or situation.

Possibility: spend a little time looking at the link provided:

https://www.themindfulnessinitiative.org/Handlers/Download. ashx?IDMF=1af56392-4cf1-4550-bdd1-72e809fa627a

Voice (of the inner critic)

Do not merely listen to the word, and so deceive yourselves. Do what it says. Anyone who listens to the word but does not do what it says is like someone who looks at his face in a mirror and, after looking at her/himself, goes away and immediately forgets what she/he looks like.

James 1 v 22

Then you will know the truth, and the truth will set you free.

John 8 v 32

Even if I should choose to boast I would not be a fool, because I would be speaking the truth. But I refrain, so no one will think more of me than is warranted by what I do or say, or because of these surpassingly great revelations. Therefore, in order to keep me from becoming conceited, I was given a thorn in my flesh, to torment me.

2 Corinthians 12 v 6–7

The power is in you. The answer is in you. You are the goal. You are the answer. It is never outside you.

Eckhart Tolle

If God had wanted me otherwise, he would have created me otherwise.

Johann Wolfgang von Goethe

January is the month when many people enrol at a gym. The excess eating over the Christmas break persuades many people to take out membership. Much is written about the percentage of people who have given up going to the gym by February. One article that I saw online suggests that about a quarter of the UK has a gym membership, but just over one in ten go regularly. A surprising number don't go at all and continue to pay. And what is it that persuades people to go in the first place? A visit to the bathroom scales or a look in the mirror? Either of which can set the inner voice (critic) chattering at the start of any New Year.

We, each one of us, has a race marked out for us (2 Timothy 4 v 7). The race marked out is probably not as an Olympic athlete, it may not be as a concert pianist, and it may not be as amazing public speaker. Depending on our stage of life, we can all have reasonable aspirations. One of these aspirations might be to just do well where you are and with what you are. This might be as a charity volunteer, a grandparent who helps out each week or a role of carer for elderly parents. One of the main discoveries that I have made is just how powerful the 'voice of inner critic' can be in the lives of many people. Often this means people believing themselves to be inferior to the person that they live with. But it can also be that you feel inferior to the person that you think you ought to be, want to be, or are expected to by others. It can be really difficult to cope with the expectations of ourselves. Even when we know grace and love from God, the inner critic can still be whispering sometimes quite incessantly that we *could* have been better, or even worse, that we *should* have been better.

Currently there are so many books, YouTube videos and magazines, which make suggestions as to how we might be better, more or different. How we might live better, own more things, holiday in wonderful locations. Social media with its airbrushed photographs increases the pressure, particularly on young women and adolescent girls. These suggestions all add to the weight of expectation in all our lives. And these suggestions can often cause us to be separate from God and from the abundant life that Jesus wants us to have.

The voice of the inner critic can also operate in our spiritual lives. It is distressing and heart-breaking when you hear about the difficulties experienced due to our inner critical voice in the realm of failure of a person's spiritual and faith life. I found this the case especially during the early days of being a Christian in my late teens and early twenties. Many other church people had strong views about what a Christian should be and expressed strong criticism of others for not following their pattern. When you are new to faith and during periods of uncertainty and doubt, it is all too easy to internalise these other voices and then add your own critical voice in a bid to live up to what others think! This is not what Jesus wants from us. In fact, it is the exact opposite. Jesus wants us to have life, abundant life (zest), where we can discover ourselves as our true selves in God. And when we do, what a transformation, what an effective antidote to the inner critic of our spiritual lives.

At the start of the mindfulness journey, the inner noise might appear deafening. This is because having allowed and listened to the inner voice day after day, month after month, year after year, it has become such a habit and loud. So, as a person starts on a mindfulness journey, they become aware of how active and persistent this noise has been. As we seek silence, as we seek peace, as we seek calm the noise can sometimes be overwhelming. And why? Because there is a lot at stake here for the ego.

The inner critic can be particularly noisy and persistent during times when you are seeking to have a time of mindful meditation. These are times when you hope for great peace and calm, but instead in the silence there is inner chatter. The inner critic saying 'you're not very good at this' or 'you're easily distracted' or 'is three minutes all you can manage!'. Therefore, mindful meditation gets added to the list of failures! A good number of other people have said this is their experience. The possible danger is that the chatter becomes louder and persuades a person to give up along this path. They give up discovering the joy and release that a mindful Christian life can bring. The pearl of great value is lost.

Possibility: it is estimated that on average we speak 7,000 words per day (some estimates much higher) but our internal voice produces many thousands more! Spend a few minutes, seeking to notice how many are neutral and how many are emotionally charged.

aVoidance (and Vulnerability)

Then he began to teach them that the Son of Man must undergo great suffering, and be rejected by the elders, the chief priests, and the scribes, and be killed, and after three days rise again. He said all this quite openly. And Peter took him aside and began to rebuke him. But turning and looking at his disciples, he rebuked Peter and said, 'Get behind me, Satan! For you are setting your mind not on divine things but on human things.'
Mark 8 v 29–33

'Truly I tell you,' Jesus answered, 'today, yes, today, before the rooster crows twice you yourself will disown me three times.'
Immediately the rooster crowed the second time. Then Peter remembered the word Jesus had spoken to him. And he broke down and wept.
Mark 14 v 30, 72

Do your best to present yourself to God as one approved, a worker who does not need to be ashamed and who correctly handles the word of truth.
2 Timothy 2 v 15

To love is to be vulnerable.
CS Lewis

Fruitfulness comes from vulnerability, and the admission of our own weakness.
Henry Nouwen

For many people it is really difficult to undo the habits of aVersion and aVoidance. It is something that has been practised for many years, and in some cases since childhood. For each one of us the things that we are vulnerable to, which we are averse to, or that we avoid can be quite different.

Some examples might include: making a decision, avoiding any kind of conflict and speaking in public. As children, we avoid some things but are encouraged to do them by our parents. We then learn the great benefits of doing so. An example might be cleaning teeth – some children really avoid this but are encouraged to do it by their parents, hopefully with careful explanation of just how beneficial this will be.

I believe that this avoidance and aversion can sometimes be tied up with vulnerability. Aversion and avoidance can easily get tied up with fear of judgement by others and self-judgement. The encouraging thing is that we are not alone. There are many people who avoid things or situations. They may be different but they may be just as painful and hard as the things you are avoiding. When we look to the Bible, we can see that there are many examples of aversion or avoidance. God has great plans for Moses. However, Moses has great plans as to how he might avoid them! When Moses is called, he puts his brother Aaron forward, rather than himself, as a person to do the work of God. He is vulnerable and fearful. Likewise, God has great plans for Jonah. When Jonah is called to go in a particular direction to Nineveh, he avoids doing so and chooses to go in the opposite direction.

In the New Testament, Paul talks about not doing the very thing that he would/should do, and doing the very thing he should not do (Romans 7 v 18). The most obvious example in the New Testament of avoidance takes place in Mark chapter 8. This chapter is the 'hinge point' of this gospel. It has a real high when Peter says to Jesus, 'You are the Christ' (Mark 8 v 29). This is, however, immediately followed by a real low, a significant attempt of aversion by Peter (Mark 8 v 32) as he tries to suggest to Jesus that he should not move towards the cross. Jesus rebukes Peter in a very strong way (Get behind me, Satan). Peter is feeling very vulnerable, he is seeking to avoid the outcome, as he believes it is going to be horrendous. Of course, Peter at this stage does not realise how glorious the outcome will be.

Later, Peter in his vulnerability, seeks to avoid outcomes to himself as well. His denial of Jesus three times (Mark 14 v 31 and 72) before the cock crows is such a well-known sequence of events. And why? Why does Peter deny Jesus three times? His avoidance, even before the most lowly of people, a serving girl, is to do with fear and anxiety. Likewise, we all have our vulnerabilities, we all have things that we find difficult to face, we all have things that we seek to avoid, and these are also driven by fear and anxiety. A mixture of past and future. Past experiences create fears deep inside us. We also have a fear of consequences in the future. Avoidance often involves ego or self-esteem. The ego is very poor at admitting that we are helpless and vulnerable.

Living in the present moment can certainly help with avoidance and aversion. Week five Mindfulness A Practical Guide to Finding Peace in a Frantic World course* is about turning towards difficulties. Our natural instinct, especially when we are low and vulnerable, when faced with difficulties, is to push them away and turn from them. The phrase 'burying our head in the sand' comes to mind. What an awkward and difficult thing that must be to try and do literally. And yet, that kind of contortion is effectively what we try to do. When we avoid adverse situations, we learn the habit and do this time and again; at the same time avoiding remembering that it didn't work the last time we tried this tactic! Einstein observed the pointlessness of repeatedly doing the same thing and expecting a different outcome. The outcome will be the same. Burying our head in the sand has the same outcome each time.

Eventually, however, things come to a point when something

different has to happen. Letting ourselves be and feel vulnerable can help us to see things differently and, allows us to focus on the things that really matter. Mindfulness can help us come to the point of acceptance, the point of change, the point of compassion. Mindfulness allows us to make a choice; it allows us to have a *metanoia* moment.

Possibility: consider how choices might be liberating: as the power to create ourselves as the unique person you are truly meant to be.

Waking Up (to the present moment)

So do not worry about tomorrow, for tomorrow will bring worries of its own. Today's trouble is enough for today.
Matthew 6 v 34

For in him we live and move and have our being.
Acts 17 v 28

Be alert and of sober mind. Your enemy the devil prowls around like a roaring lion looking for someone to devour.
1 Peter 5 v 8

I can't go back to yesterday, because I was a different person then.
Lewis Carroll

The most important hour is always the present.
Meister Eckhart

Just for a moment consider these two short sentences. God is nowhere. God is now here. The sentences contain the same letters and in the same order. The only difference between the two sentences is that there is a space in the word nowhere, creating two words now here. And this character space transforms the sentence. This moment of space in our lives can transform our characters. This space is the difference between God being nowhere in our lives and being now and here in our lives. Meister Eckhart* wrote 'there is but one now'. And in each of these now moments we need to wake up.

All our yesterdays have been a series of present moments. Many thousands of them! But they are all yesterdays, and gone. All our tomorrows will offer us a series of present moments.

Again, thousands of them! But we haven't arrived there yet. And so, patience is required to be in each of our current present moments. Fretting about what happened yesterday or what might happen tomorrow are all obstacles to being in the present moment. Fretting about what happened earlier today or what might happen later today or tonight are all obstacles to being in the present moment. Waking up to the present moment gives us freedom. Freedom from the past and its problems and freedom from the future with its imagined outcomes. As we slip back into the past, or, start to move into the future, then we begin to lose this freedom and we lose our peace.

Each present moment is a chance to wake up, a moment to begin again. Each present moment is a chance to wake up and connect again to the presence of God's love. If only we allow it. God gives us sufficient grace to live in the present moment, and not be slipping backwards and forwards in time. Accepting what is, rather than struggling and stressing into trying to make it something else, somewhere else. It is this struggling and stressing that tires us out. If we are able to be in the present moment, this is where we can learn, where we can gain insight and where we might receive guidance. It is almost as if we are between two giant magnets. The first magnet is seeking to draw us back in time to the past, the second magnet is seeking to draw us forward into the future. Our aim in life, is somehow to resist the pull of both of these powerful magnets.

The story of the creation in Genesis, in whichever form you understand the story, is marked out in single days. In each day of creation as described in Genesis, God carries out an action. In the Godly play version of the story, participants are encouraged to consider the events of each day. Participants are also requested to consider which day matters the least? A very challenging question! For us, in the twenty-first century, each day matters. We are called to enjoy each and every day, and within that single day, enjoy as many single moments as we are able to.

There is a wonderful book by Christophe Andre* which explores art and mindfulness. In this book there is a lovely picture of a snow scene which includes in it a blackbird. As we look at the picture, we are reminded that it is a picture of a single moment. In the next moment, things will be different. The blackbird may or may not be there, and even if it is there, it will be a tiny bit different in its posture and its appearance, and in its life. If we sit and gaze out of the window, then any given scene that we are looking at will change from moment to moment. As I write this sentence, there is no snow, there is sunshine and there is a breeze. And in that breeze, the trees, bushes and plants are in constant motion. In that breeze, the light and the shadows are likewise in constant motion. Each and every moment is unique. The last present moment has already passed. The next present moment has not happened yet, and, it may never be in the way imagined or planned. The only moment is this present moment, and it is in this present moment that we need to wake up and be alert.

Many years ago, I took a series of Alexander Technique lessons. In some ways, the Alexander Technique bears similarities to the mindfulness body scan by bringing great awareness to the breath and to the body (and most especially the neck, which is where Alexander himself discovered that he was carrying the most tension). My teacher would often use the phrase 'end-gaining'. End-gaining was her description of jumping ahead to a hoped-for outcome. This process of end-gaining was the very opposite of mindfully waking up to being in the present moment.

Possibility: watch on Youtube Jason Mraz 'Living in the moment' official video.

Worry

Who of you by worrying can add a single hour to your life?
Since you cannot do this very little thing, why do you worry
about the rest?
Luke 12 v 25–26

Cast all your anxiety on Him, because he cares for you.
1 Peter 5 v 7

You would not worry so much about what others think of
you, if you realised how seldom they do.
Eleanor Roosevelt

Alice: This is impossible. The Mad Hatter: Only if you believe
it is.
Lewis Carroll

In the *Peanuts* cartoon, there is the brilliant line: 'Don't worry
about tomorrow, it is already today in Australia.' Very little
improves by worrying about it. I know this. You know this.
However, most people don't know this. A big percentage of
what each person worries about never happens.

I cannot think of anything that has improved by me worrying
about it. I know logically there is no point in worrying. But
sometimes logic is overtaken by emotion.

Many years ago, I was invited by two former residents
of the Müller children's homes in Bristol to look around. It
is now a museum which welcomes visitors from all over
the world. George Müller, who himself lived rent free in an
orphanage for two months, housed and educated over 10,000
orphans. He did this through prayer, faith and the generosity
of thousands. On the visit, I was very much struck by how

Müller had not seemed to worry – even, for example, when the heating broke down in the midst of winter. Miraculously, and literally miraculously, there was a brief intermission in the cold weather while the heating was fixed. Even in the difficult times, Müller seemed to be able to live in the present, and, instead of worrying, had a deep trust in God. By shifting focus from the thing or the person causing us to worry to a trust in Jesus, changes happen. Jesus knows that not only is worry not good for us, but actually, that worry is bad for us! Jesus says in the Sermon on the Mount that it will be detrimental to our health and shorten our lives.

Over-attachment can lead to worry. We worry about not having things, things going wrong, the cost of things. We worry about the things that we say, and things we do not get around to saying. We worry about what is communicated and what is not communicated. And in all these worries, we get distracted, distracted away from the presence of God. We get distracted from the care and love of other people. We get distracted from the whole wonderful beautiful world around us. Worry is a sign that we are relying on ourselves, our own skills and abilities, instead of the resources that God wants to offer us.

I have seen it written in a number of places that a tendency to worry has got something to do with our genes – that 'we are simply wired that way'. If this is true, then it makes it harder for those at the end of the spectrum who have been 'wired-in' worriers. Augustine* thought about and wrote about, self-awareness. However, despite huge successes, Augustine was himself prone to worry. He was dissatisfied with his life. One thing to learn from this is not to worry, or waste energy, by seeking to compare yourself with others and whoever you are or hope to be. God understands us and loves us whether we worry a lot, or, whether we worry just a little.

Corrie ten Boom said that worry does not empty tomorrow of

its sorrows, it only empties today of its strength. Each day we live is the tomorrow of yesterday. We have a choice each and every day, whether we try to live today's tomorrow today or when it happens, i.e., tomorrow. I know that sounds really complicated, but trying to worry one day ahead is just that: worry. We usually do not have all the information or knowledge needed about tomorrow, so why beat ourselves up today? Planning ahead and worrying ahead are very different activities. Planning ahead is good, worrying ahead is bad!

Some people argue that a small amount of anxiety is a helpful and desirable thing. It is argued, for example, that the anxiety will ensure that you get certain things done which are obligations or legal requirements. However, what can happen for some of us, or indeed all of us, is that the anxiety becomes exaggerated by worry. In other words, the worry has magnified and multiplied the original anxiety. A particular example might be applying for a promotion. The original worry of whether you get the promotion or not can be escalated and exaggerated into other thoughts such as: What will my work colleagues think of me, how will my children react, I'm such a failure, how will we manage all our household bills? This kind of exaggeration and escalation is not in any way helpful, so our logical minds will inform us of this and yet, it can still happen!

Mindfulness, being in the present, helps a lot with dealing with worry. Much worry has its roots in the past – things which have happened, things which have gone wrong, things which were said. And these things are then projected into the future, together with an unhealthy mix of desire, fear and distortion. The present provides freedom from such recalling from the past and projecting forward into the future. Coming back to the present, coming back to oneself, coming back to the breath, coming back to the body are needed. All of these things will help greatly but all of these things require great effort, great discipline and great practice. We need to remember though that all of these things help to gain freedom from worry.

Possibility: you could try setting an alarm each hour or for certain times a day and just see what you are doing, how you are feeling, whether you are worrying, when the alarm goes off. Are you present in that moment?

eXperiential

The Word became flesh and made his dwelling among us. We have seen his glory, the glory of the one and only Son, who came from the Father, full of grace and truth.
John 1 v 14

But when the set time had fully come, God sent his Son, born of a woman.
Galatians 4 v 4

Rather, he made himself nothing by taking the very nature of a servant, being made in human likeness. And being found in appearance as a man, he humbled himself.
Philippians 2 v 7–8

I don't make plans. I live my life on a daily basis.
Paulo Coelho

The price of inaction is far greater than the cost of making a mistake.
Meister Eckhart

I nearly made the title of this section Xenon. But then I thought it might prompt readers who had very little interest in chemistry to skip the section altogether. Nevertheless, there is good reason for including just a little information about Xenon. Xenon is a chemical element with the symbol Xe and atomic number 54 and was discovered by William Ramsay and Morris Travers in 1898. Xenon comes from the Greek word for stranger. Xenon is a colourless, dense, odourless noble gas found in Earth's atmosphere in trace amounts. It is used in two ways: in flash lamps and as a general anaesthetic. One of xenon's most important properties is its inertness. If you breathe pure xenon, it'll drive out all the oxygen and kill you!

In this section about the experiential nature of mindfulness, I would like to draw out from my description of Xenon a couple of key points. Firstly, that mindfulness requires us not to be inert. On the contrary it requires us to be attentive, alert and active. Secondly, what we might discover is that some elements of ourselves are a 'stranger'. Because of our habits, our thought patterns and the temptation to live in the past or in the future all come together to make our very deepest, innermost being a stranger to us.

Christian contemplatives have been aware of the importance of body position on the effectiveness of their meditation and prayer. The initiator of the Alexander technique was himself an actor who found that his performances were adversely affected by constriction in his throat. He realised that there was an interaction between his mind and body. The NHS website says this: 'The Alexander Technique teaches improved posture and movement, which is believed to help reduce and prevent problems caused by unhelpful habits. During lessons you are taught to be more aware of your body, how to improve poor posture and move more efficiently. Teachers of the Alexander Technique believe it helps get rid of tension in your body and relieves problems such as back pain, neck ache, sore shoulders and other musculoskeletal problems.'

One of the things that Alexander teachers encourage is to imagine having a string from the top of your head reaching upwards to the ceiling. The purpose of this imagining is to experience the lightness of the head resting on the shoulders and neck. Alexander himself had experienced the benefits of doing this. Reading about doing this would do one thing – fill the mind with how in theory this might work. Actually doing this, is quite another thing – it gives a person the experience of what it is like, how it feels, and some measure of the benefits of doing it. Reading about something and doing that same thing are quite different, with different outcomes and benefits.

During the coronavirus lockdown, when so many people were fearful about their mental health, one of the significant changes that took place in the country was the reconnection between people and gardens and people with nature. The purchasing of seeds online grew exponentially. The experience of planting seeds, and nurturing young plants, became for many people a way of coping. Reading about gardening, watching YouTube how-to videos is no substitute for the experiential nature of the fresh air, the feel of compost and soil or the satisfaction of clearing weeds.

It is time to reconnect the spiritual with the bodily, and the bodily with the spiritual. This 'dualism', has evolved over many centuries but is quite unhelpful. Mindfulness is experiential. It involves the body as well as the mind. It involves the breath, as well as the mind. It involves mind, breath and body all in the present moment. The body is always a grounding place in God's presence in this world. In John's Gospel (John 1 v 14): 'The word became flesh and dwelt among us.' Jesus experienced the human, bodily form (Philippians 2 v 7).

Our own lives are so complex, deep and mysterious. How could we possibly imagine that someone (other than God) could know me better than I know myself (and conversely, how could I be so arrogant to think that I fully comprehend the meaning of someone else's life)? How can I possibly imagine that anyone else could carry out the experiential life of me?

This experiential life of me needs to be full of self-compassion. And this self-compassion must allow me to say yes when I, not others, believe that the answer is yes. Similarly, this self-compassion must allow me to say no when I, not others, believe that the answer is no. What an amazing freedom this kind of self-compassion will imbibe into this experiential life. Freedom to say yes and to say no. Freedom not to be afraid of other people. Freedom not to be afraid of fear.

Possibility: spend a few moments both sitting and standing, and testing out the Alexander Technique notion of imagining a piece of string attached to the top of your head, allowing a lightness of your head on your shoulders. Reflect on how this feels.

eXtrovert/introvert

Be careful not to practise your righteousness in front of others
to be seen by them. If you do, you would have no reward in
heaven. So, when you give to the needy, do not announce it
with trumpets as the hypocrites do, to be honoured by others.
Matthew 6 v 1–2

Everything they do is done for people to see... they love to be
greeted with respect in the market-places.
Matthew 23 v 5, 7

People who don't think, shouldn't talk.
Lewis Carroll

Never miss an opportunity to shut up.
Mark Twain

As I have been practising mindfulness over the past few years, I
have become more alert to the two personality types which are
commonly called, or labelled, introverts and extroverts. I have
tried to consider whether mindfulness might be different for
these two groups of people. It may be that you have considered
the question whether Christian spirituality might be different for
introverts and extroverts. Maybe you consider these questions
to be too simplistic and possibly even irrelevant? I think it may
be helpful to just give this some consideration. Being extrovert
does not make you the same as all other extroverts. Being
introvert does not make you the same as all other introverts.
Myers-Briggs* uses the introvert and extrovert scale as one of
the four basic divisions of personality types.

Some would like to suggest that Jesus was an extrovert, a
party person, a person with a group of followers and a person

who performs miracles in front of thousands. Others would like to suggest that Jesus was an introvert, a person who prays on his own away from others, reflects deeply, and teaches one to one with key characters in the gospel story. I am not sure that Jesus can be categorised that easily as either extrovert or introvert. And I am not sure that we, each one of us, can be categorised that easily either. It may be that in certain circumstances, we may be on one part of the introvert/extrovert scale, but then in other scenarios, have attributes from the other part of the scale? Wherever we may be on the scale, there is a place in God's Kingdom for both extroverts and introverts – of this, I am sure.

When considering whether mindfulness might be different for these two groups of people, one topic to give attention to is that introverts have a lower threshold for noise and stimulation, whereas extroverts have a much higher threshold. This has an impact on the 'sounds meditation', where students are invited to focus on sounds. Before jumping to any conclusions, I would like to suggest that despite the lower or higher thresholds, that it is possible for both groups of people to be attentive to sounds, distracted by sounds, add 'stories' to the sounds that they hear.

My observation has been that introverts are attentive, listen well, notice, and are often slow to speak. This is not because they are afraid or because they are dull or unintelligent, but because they are reflective and careful. It might almost appear to some that they are disinterested. I believe this to be far from the case. Conversely, my observation has been that extroverts reflect less and are happier to process out loud in front of others. This might be because maybe words are less permanent for them and they have less sensitivity to what is said and what impact this may have on other people.

Viktor Frankl* wrote a little bit about stimulus and the response to the stimulus. He suggested that between the stimulus and response there is a space, and in that space, is when we make our choices. I believe that mindfulness helps us lengthen that space. And by lengthening that space, this can lead to us making different, and hopefully better, responses to situations. By lengthening that space between the stimulus and response, this hopefully provides us with more freedom to be our unique and wonderful selves and to have the potential to show more kindness to others.

Some psychologists suggest that it is hard to change our very basic personality traits. Some Christian writers and speakers would disagree. We can turn to the example of Paul and his Damascus Road experience of dramatic change. Whether or not you agree that significant change can, or might, or will happen in our lives as we draw closer to God, what is clear is the following: that by understanding our personality traits, and by not constraining ourselves to any particular categories (through the use of enneagrams or Myers-Briggs testing, for example), we can live our lives more abundantly. By being open hearted, willing to embrace change, and not being too self-judgemental, and having a beginner's mind, then new possibilities emerge and arrive.

People sometimes worry that they are missing out because of the type of people that they are. This may be more common among introverts (I am one!), who believe if only they were more outgoing, more gregarious and more sociable then it might somehow be different. It may of course be that extroverts feel like they're missing out. Missing out on the more sensitive and caring and content contemplative side of faith and life. But we all need each other, introverts and extroverts. We are all interdependent, all loved by God just as we are. Our different personalities go to make up the stained glass window. When the light shines through, it only makes sense when all the colours and pieces are there.

Possibility: in one study quoted in Quiet by Susan Cain (p. 124), extroverts chose a background noise level of 72 decibels and introverts 55 decibels (compared with a smoke alarm which is 85 decibels). Take a few moments to consider what this means.

You and Mindfulness

...to put off your old self, which is being corrupted by its deceitful desires; to be made new in the attitude of your minds; and to put on the new self, created to be like God in true righteousness and holiness.
Ephesians 4 v 22–24

Therefore, if anyone is in Christ, the new creation has come: the old has gone, the new is here!
2 Corinthians 5 v 17

You must live in the present, launch yourself on every wave, find your eternity in each moment.
Henry David Thoreau

Mindfulness is the miracle by which we master and restore ourselves.
Thich Nhat Hanh

It may be that you have worked through this book methodically, reading it from A to Z. If yes, then thank you so much for persevering, and arriving at the letter Y, which will hopefully help YOU.

It may also be that you have randomly selected words, dotted around in the book and not read it systematically, and, that you might have started with this particular word YOU as an interesting place to start. In which case I very much hope that you will be tempted to carry on reading the book and randomly selecting words that you might find helpful and speak into your current situation.

However, of course 'YOU', is a very interesting place to begin when considering mindfulness.

What I believe to be true is that mindfulness can be very helpful, beneficial and life changing for YOU!

Mindfulness is available to you and every person, every person that has breath. Whatever your background, age, nationality, political interests, wealth, whatever your spiritual or faith background, whatever type of Christian you might consider yourself to be, mindfulness has the potential to help you. It has the potential to help you become more patient, more compassionate to yourself, more compassionate to other people, perhaps calmer, less stressed, have more zest and many other things. What mindfulness will certainly do is facilitate the possibility that you will not spend your time wishing you were somewhere else, wishing you were somebody else, wishing you were something else. Mindfulness will help you more readily accept the person that you are, unique, special, and more aware of just how loved you are.

I once read about an experiment that was carried out in a church. In that church, the congregation were asked to close their eyes and answer two questions. While all eyes were closed, no one could see how any individual person answered either of the two questions. The first invitation was to raise their hand to the question 'do you believe you are loved by God?'.

A significant percentage of people raised their hands. The congregation was then asked to put their hands down. Then the second question was asked. The second invitation was to raise their hand to the question 'do you believe you are liked by God?'. And what do you think might have happened? Well, the answer is that the percentage number of hands that were raised for the second request was very much lower. And why was there such a difference? The answer is probably quite complex. But I would guess that among that congregation, it had something to do with self-acceptance, something to do with perhaps not understanding grace, something to do with failing to understand themselves.

My experience has been that some people have turned to mindfulness in the hope that it will create a new person, 'a new you'. Mindfulness is sometimes likened to a fitness programme in the gym, with the aim of losing weight in a certain period of time. In the same way, some students of mindfulness anticipate that after a certain number of weeks of mindfulness they would become a new de-stressed person. But it isn't quite like this. Certainly, it may be true that many people do become calmer or less stressed, but this should not be your main aim. Meister Eckhart,* counters the notion of going on a mindfulness spiritual journey as linear. By this he meant that a person sets out by doing 20 minutes meditation a day and at the end of six months that they will be 40% less stressed, and after 12 months that they will be 80% less stressed. Rather, what can happen is that you are indeed less stressed. But this is a by-product of something even more significant: through mindfulness, by being with yourself, noticing, drinking deeply from the well of your existing spirituality, you discover more YOUness. How wonderful!

When we practise something, we get better at it. So if we practise kindness, we get better at it.

If we practise grumpiness, we get better at it. If you practise mindfulness, you will get better at it. But, with YOU and mindfulness there are: no time scales, no linear progress to achieve, no pressure to achieve anything at all. You are not here for worldly achievement alone. You are here for something far more. Rumi* is quoted as saying, 'Yesterday I was clever, so I wanted to change the world. Today I am wise, so I am changing myself.' I would like to suggest that you are wise if you are becoming more yourself, more YOU.

Possibility: perhaps say a short prayer to thank God that I am loved and liked by God, and practise this prayer for the rest of this week.

You and the Future

I consider that our present sufferings are not worth comparing with the glory that will be revealed in us.

Romans 8 v 18

Do not be afraid of those who kill the body, but cannot kill the soul.

Matthew 10 v 28

And certainly you know, it's time to start something new and trust the magic of beginnings.

Meister Eckhart

Your time is limited, so don't waste it living someone else's life. Don't be trapped by dogma – which is living with the results of other people's thinking. Don't let the noise of other's opinions drown out your own inner voice. And most important, have the courage to follow your heart and intuition. They somehow already know what you truly want to become. Everything else is secondary.

Steve Jobs

As you go on your way, there is no life map with all the landmarks clearly in place. Life has not happened yet. The landmarks may yet to be formed. No one has gone on your particular and unique life journey before. No one has had to make your life decisions in exactly the same way.

The only world expert on you is you. Your parents, siblings, spouse or partner may have lots of the pieces of the jigsaw puzzle, but they do not have the full picture. Any one of them may have opinions, sometimes strong opinions, about what is right for you. But their opinions are based on only some of the pieces of the jigsaw puzzle.

There are many guides which might help us through this journey – poetry, art, music, nature, all there to help us see the picture of our own lives. All of these might help us step forward in ignorance and hope, imagination and anticipation, trust and faith. And the amazing thing is, we can change the route as we discover more! We need to remain open if we are to make the most of a journey. To the left of us, and to the right of us, there may be waterfalls, beautiful birds, rugged outcrops and a whole host of other beautiful and wonderful experiences. Staying on the tarmac road, without imagination, without spontaneity, without insight will result in disappointment. We will not be on the path to the abundant life that is available to us. And it may be that now, or at some point in the future, mindfulness can help you explore these points of beauty, these moments of imagination, these times of flourishing rather than worrying.

Do not be afraid. Be yourself, and not what others expect of you. At the right time, which may be now, allow mindfulness to help you in your physical and spiritual life development and exploration. See how wonderful, how marvellous, how affirming this might be. Don't be afraid of yourself and all the complexity and complications that Mindfulness shows you about yourself.

The gospel description of the Road to Emmaus is a wonderful story from which we can all learn.

In the first part of the narrative, there is great uncertainty, worry, questioning and sorrow. The couple walking on the road is frightened and have no idea what the future holds. And then everything changes, their eyes are opened, fear turns to joy, uncertainty turns to possibility, fear turns to courage. And when their eyes are opened, they see that Jesus is the saviour, perhaps not quite in the same way that they had anticipated, but even more powerfully because of this. There are times in our lives when our eyes are not open, when we cannot see, when we cannot appreciate or understand. But this wonderful passage demonstrates that our eyes can be opened.

In Peter Lupson's book *God's Company*, he describes the life journeys of seven Christian entrepreneurs/businessmen including William Colgate, Henry Heinz and James Kraft. In each of these life stories, being open to changes of direction play an important part in what they become. Having trust and faith in God plays an even more important part. Each of the businessmen described, goes on to make a huge fortune. But more importantly, each one fulfils the life journey that presents itself. In all cases they are honest and true in their business lives, and ultimately very generous in all kinds of ways with the proceeds of their businesses.

For YOU, here are some possibilities for the future:

https://www.nhs.uk/apps-library/be-mindful/ is an app available from the NHS. It costs £30. I have not personally used this app, but because it is provided by the NHS, I would hope it is comprehensive, reliable and helpful.

https://www.nhs.uk/conditions/stress-anxiety-depression/improve-mental-wellbeing/ is a 5-step programme, again available from the NHS

It suggests: connecting to others
being physically active
learning new skills
giving to others
mindfulness (pay attention to the present moment)

The headspace app is very popular. Available through Google Play Store and Apple. Also, online Headspace.co.uk

At the end of the book, I have listed some books which may

be good starting points for the next steps of your Christian Mindfulness journey. These are all books that I have read, and all books that I have benefitted from.

Mindfulness is, however, not just a theory but an experience. And if the time is right an accredited Mindfulness A Practical Guide to Finding Peace in a Frantic World course*is a significant way to make progress. the reason I say 'if the time is right', is because occasionally the time may not be quite right. And it may be better to delay slightly until the time is right. If you suffer from any particular mental health issues, then it would be good to discuss the possibility of a mindfulness course with your GP or mental health specialist. It would also be very sensible to advise the mindfulness teacher of your particular condition(s). Have a look at the Oxford Mindfulness Centre website for possibilities of courses and accredited teachers. The website also provides lots of other information. Whatever you choose to do, or choose not to do next, be kind to yourself!

Possibility: what might you do next? Jot down your intention. And jot down a possible timescale.

Zest (or abundant life)

I have come that you may have life, and have it to the full.
John 10 v 10

I can do all this through him who gives me strength.
Philippians 4 v 13

Life is enthusiasm, zest.
Laurence Olivier

Zest is the secret of all beauty. There is no beauty that is attractive, without zest.
Christian Dior

In the dictionary, zest has two meanings. The first meaning is the outer part of citrus fruit, used as flavouring. The second meaning is having great enthusiasm and energy. Jesus wants to add flavouring to our lives, He wants to give us great enthusiasm and energy, He promises us life in abundance! This is not just a possibility but a promise. How wonderful, how marvellous, how affirming. And if it is a promise rather than just a possibility, then why do we accept anything less?

Why do we need to just struggle along, just make do when instead, we can be 'flavoured' by Jesus, to live abundantly full of energy and enthusiasm? We can go on a journey of exploration, imagination, growth, living in the present and also in the eternal. DH Lawrence suggested that 'the living self has one purpose, to come into its own being, as a tree comes into blossom'.

If you speak to secular people, who have very little concept of the gospel story, and you ask them the question 'would you like to have abundant life?', then I feel confident that many would say 'yes' straight away. And then, if you offered them some supplementary information, suggesting that 'this abundant life is available every day, every moment of every day' and then asked them again 'would you like to have abundant life?', well, then the yes would surely be an even more emphatic one. But what does it really mean to have abundant life? I am sure it does NOT mean a life full of material possessions (although some Christians that I have met have a kind of theology of materialism which suggests this might be the case). Abundant life does not mean a life of ease, a life where all goes well, a life when you have all the material possessions that you could dream of. Abundant life does not relate directly to the material circumstances that we find ourselves in. The source of this zest, this abundant life is not outside of us. But deep within us. It is part of our very essence of who we are. Zest can develop. And then from deep within us, the way we look at things starts to be different. When we change the way we look at things, the things we look at change. And as we do this, change happens: to ourselves, to our lives which become more fuller, more flavoured and more enriched.

Abundant life is a life lived in the present moment, in the presence of Jesus, where our attitude to what is happening plays a part in receiving that abundant life from Jesus. So, the flavouring requires that we are present. The flavouring requires that part of our attitude is gratitude. Then we come to experience the spiritual life, the life of love, joy, peace, patience, kindness, goodness, faithfulness, gentleness and self-control (Galatians 5 v 22–23).

The Christian life has been distorted and constrained by so many people over so many years. Constrained into a set of rules, distorted into trying to get a healthy balance of more rights than wrongs, where there are more credits than debits in anticipation of the final reckoning. This does not strike me as life lived in abundance – a life of abundant joy, abundant love and abundant spiritual fire. This abundant life is a miracle, but then, Jesus is in the business of miracles – loaves and fishes, healings, restoration to life.

This abundant life takes place in the ordinary everyday events of our lives. And for the great majority of us as Christians, there are many more ordinary moments each day than extraordinary moments, many more routine moments than epiphanies, many more moments of walking along the paths of our ordinary existence, rather than being on the road to Damascus. And for most other people this is also true. They have far more ordinary moments than extraordinary moments. So, in our ordinary moments, and in their ordinary moments, and where these intersect, this is the time when we can have the abundant life that we are promised. In other words, all of the time! The potential and possibility are there for the whole of our lives, each and every one of us. So even if we wish to do extraordinary things, like climb Mount Everest, or walk around the circumference of the earth, this will be achieved with a whole succession of ordinary moments. The first steps start at our front door. One step at a time. And in each one of these steps, we connect to the source of all life and light and being. We connect to ourselves and to each other. We connect to more zest and abundance of life in each moment, each day.

Possibility: think ahead to one 'ordinary' thing that you will do today, and consider how you might approach that activity. Might there be a sense of abundant life as you undertake that activity?

Zacchaeus

Jesus entered Jericho and was passing through. A man was there by the name of Zacchaeus; he was a chief tax collector and was wealthy. He wanted to see who Jesus was, but because he was short, he could not see over the crowd. So he ran ahead and climbed a sycamore-fig tree to see him, since Jesus was coming that way.
When Jesus reached the spot, he looked up and said to him, 'Zacchaeus, come down immediately. I must stay at your house today.' So he came down at once and welcomed him gladly. All the people saw this and began to mutter, 'He has gone to be the guest of a sinner.' But Zacchaeus stood up and said to the Lord, 'Look, Lord! Here and now, I give half of my possessions to the poor, and if I have cheated anybody out of anything, I will pay back four times the amount.' Jesus said to him, 'Today salvation has come to this house, because this man, too, is a son of Abraham. For the Son of Man came to seek and to save the lost.'
Luke 19 v 1–10

Change will not come if we wait for some other person or some other time. We are the ones we have been waiting for. We are the change that we seek.
Barack Obama

The greatest tragedy in life is to spend your whole life at fishing, only to discover, it was never fish that you were after.
Henry David Thoreau

The story of Zacchaeus is a well-known Sunday school (young church) story. In Sunday school, the focus is often on Zacchaeus being a short man, who because of his short stature, needs to climb the tree to be noticed. Zacchaeus knows that he needs to climb the tree and knows that it is now or never. If he climbs the tree now, he has got a chance to see Jesus. If he doesn't climb the tree, then he knows that he is too short to see Jesus and there is a chance that he never will see Him.

Zacchaeus was rich. You might imagine that he had other ways of getting to see Jesus. I think there is an element of humility in the way that Zacchaeus climbs the tree, and makes it possible for the interaction to take place. But the story has other elements and can teach us so much more.

Zacchaeus tries to see Jesus. And, Jesus notices him, was mindful of him. And through that mindful observance of Zacchaeus, He brings about change. Through the interaction, the life of Zacchaeus is changed for ever. Zacchaeus is made whole and given new zest (abundant life).

One of the interesting aspects of the story of Zacchaeus is that both Zacchaeus and Jesus make the most of the present moment. Jesus calls up to Zacchaeus and says come down, for I must stay in your house, today, now. Zacchaeus comes down from the tree without hesitation. He comes down from the tree with great happiness (Luke 19 v 6). He is going to make his house available to Jesus, today, now. And the outcome? The outcome is that today, now, Jesus says to Zacchaeus 'salvation comes to this house'.

It is not about tomorrow, it is not about yesterday, it is about the very day that Jesus and Zacchaeus had the encounter. They eat and drink that day, in that present moment. No need to worry about what they will eat tomorrow (Matthew 6 v 31), indeed, no need to be anxious about tomorrow for anything. Today is the day. Today is the day of salvation, a present-day reality, a day when it will be different, when Zacchaeus will not be suffering any longer from the consequences off his greed and swindling, not be suffering any longer from loneliness.

This interaction in Luke's Gospel occurs in chapter 19.

There are only 24 chapters in Luke. This event takes place very much towards the end of the life and ministry of Jesus, as He approaches Jerusalem, the Last Supper, the crucifixion. Despite all that is on the mind of Jesus, He is looking up, He is noticing, He is aware, and is still full of compassion. Jesus sees beyond the exterior which is a swindling tax gatherer and sees to the heart of Zacchaeus.

What a fantastic story. Zacchaeus is awake, now, determined to make change in his life, he has accepted forgiveness from Jesus with gratitude. The judgement of others around him will now be different, as they see his new lifestyle; a new life of honesty and kindness. Zacchaeus will have peace his heart when he implements the return of the money that he has falsely taken.

The Rumi poem, called the 'Guest House', used in the Mindfulness A Practical Guide to Finding Peace in a Frantic World course* has a line 'Be grateful for whoever comes, because each has been sent as a guide from beyond.' The poem is talking about strangers coming, thoughts coming, difficulties coming. But here in this passage in Luke's Gospel, it is Jesus who comes, and Zacchaeus is eternally grateful.

This one incident is a turning point, a *metanoia* moment, a chance for Zacchaeus to begin again. Just as when you first came to faith. Whether in a dramatic moment, or a step in a gradual process, you will probably remember this time with great joy. Hopefully you will be able to add to this joy by taking another step forward, having another *metanoia* moment, and exploring mindfulness further in relation to your faith and spirituality. My hope is that you take the next steps forward, so that you might even more expand to be the life that God wants you to have.

Possibility: consider again the quote: 'The greatest tragedy in life is to spend your whole life at fishing, only to discover, it was never fish that you were after.' What is it that you are after?

People mentioned with an * in the text

Christophe Andre (b. 1956) is a French psychiatrist and psychotherapist who worked in the Paris University hospital service of mental health and therapeutics, specialising in depression and anxiety disorders. He has written more than 30 books, including one jointly with Mathieu Ricard.*

Augustine (354–430) was a theologian, philosopher, and bishop in North Africa (modern day Algeria). He was canonized in 1298. He was a prolific writer and his writings have been very influential in the Christian world.

Thomas Aquinas (1225–1274) was a Dominican friar, philosopher, theologian and scholar. He was the proponent of 'natural theology' and argued that reason is found in God.

Susan Cain (b. 1968) is a US writer, speaker and former lawyer. Her bestselling book *Quiet: The Power of Introverts in a World That Can't Stop Talking* was developed because of her own difficulties with public speaking. Her first TED talk video reached 1 million people more quickly than any other video.

Susan David (b. 1970) is the founder of the Institute of Coaching at the Harvard Medical School, a psychologist, keynote speaker and author of the book *Emotional Agility*. This topic she presented as a TED talk and was watched by more than 1 million people in its first week of release.

Catherine of Siena (1347–1380) was a lay member of the Dominican Order, a mystic and writer. She was declared as patron saint of Italy in 1939 and of Europe in 1970. She is considered one of the greatest female theological writers and along with Teresa of Ávila* one of the first two women to be given the title 'Doctor of the Church'.

Dalai Lama (b. 1935) describes himself as a simple Buddhist monk. Each Dalai Lama (currently he is the thirteenth in succession) is committed to helping humanity and all sentient beings. He is also committed to peace and won the Nobel peace prize in 1989. He has written many books especially about joy, happiness and wisdom.

Emily Dickinson (1830–1886) was a US poet who lived an isolated life, much of the time not leaving her house (or bedroom). She wrote an incredible 1800 poems although only 10 were published during her lifetime. Her poems have been a real inspiration to many.

Meister Eckhart (c. 1260–1327/8) was a German Dominican friar, theologian, philosopher and mystic. Little is known about his early life, but was a great scholar and writer. His writings have attracted seekers of truth among Christians and non-Christians.

John of the Cross (1542–1591) was a Spanish Carmelite friar, mystic and poet. He was mentored by Teresa of Ávila* and was influenced by Thomas Aquinas.* When imprisoned in a small windowless cell for nine months, with just a small 3-inch hole for light, he wrote *Dark Night of the Soul*, considered a spiritual masterpiece.

Julian of Norwich (c. 1342–1416), was a Christian mystic. In her equivalent of self-isolation, she explored this concept of 'oneing'. She is considered to be the first woman to write in the English language. She received, and wrote about, a series of visions that she had. Her writing is simultaneously complex and simple.

Jon Kabat-Zinn (b. 1944) is an incredibly significant person in the modern development of Mindfulness. He developed the Mindfulness Based Stress Relief (MBSR) programme at the University of Massachusetts, which has been used in many clinical settings in the UK and US.
He is the author of many books including *Wherever You Go, There You Are*.

Frigyes Karinthy (1887–1938) was a Hungarian journalist, writer and translator. His notion of 'six degrees of separation' was first set out in 1929 and popularised in a John Guare play in 1990 which explores the theme in detail. It is also known as the six handshakes rule.

RT Kendall (b. 1935) is a US Christian writer, speaker and minister. He was the minister of Westminster Chapel in London for 25 years. He has written more than 50 books.

Martin Luther King (1929–1968) was a US pastor, writer and civil rights activist. He is known for his non-violence and civil disobedience in order to further civil rights. He won the Nobel Peace Prize in 1964 and was assassinated in 1968.

Max Lucado (b. 1955) is a US pastor, author and speaker. He has written about 100 books.

Thomas Merton (1915–1968) was an American Trappist monk, writer, theologian and scholar. After a wild adolescence and youth, including a time at Cambridge University, he entered a monastery in 1941. He wrote more than 50 books, mostly on Christian spirituality, but was also interested in interfaith understanding.

Isabel Myers (1897–1980) and **Katherine Briggs** (1875–1968) formulated a questionnaire which indicated how people perceive the world and how they make decisions. The Myers-Briggs Type Indicator is one of the world's most widely used personality indicators.

Henri Nouwen (1932–1996) was a Dutch writer, theologian and Catholic priest. His work and interest combined pastoral care, social care and psychology. He was Professor of Divinity at Harvard. He wrote nearly 40 books, including *The Return of the Prodigal Son*.

Blaise Pascal (1623–1662) was a French writer, mathematician and theologian. He was one of the first two inventors of a mathematical calculator. When in his twenties, he became interested in philosophy and Catholic theology.

Mathieu Ricard (b. 1946) was born in France but has lived in the Himalayan region for 45 years. He is a Buddhist monk, photographer, translator and author of many books. His TED talks on happiness and altruism have been watched by more than 7 million people.

Richard Rohr (b. 1943) is a US Franciscan friar. In 1986, Rohr founded the Center for Action and Contemplation. He is a popular speaker and has written more than 30 books. He focusses on what we do (orthopraxis) as well as what we say (verbal orthodoxy).

Rumi (1207–1273) was a Persian poet, theologian and Sufi mystic. His very popular poetry speaks of how love infuses the world. His poetry is used in the Mindfulness A Practical Guide to Finding Peace in a Frantic World course.*

Angelus Silesius (1624–1677) was a German Catholic priest, mystic and poet. He wrote extensively, including more than 1500 poems, 200 hymns, and 50 tracts.

Teresa of Ávila (1515–1582) was a Spanish, Roman Catholic nun, the originator of the Carmelite reform, who placed great emphasis on reading and contemplation. She suggested a day spent not reading a book was a day wasted. She founded 14 monasteries and in 1577 wrote *The Interior Castle* as a guide to spiritual development.

Saint Therese (1873–1897), was a French Carmelite nun, known for her simple life and practical approach to spirituality. She has been recognised by the Catholic church as a 'Doctor of the Church', one of only four women. She is a very popular Saint and has been the inspiration for music and films. She died from TB at the age of 24.

Eckhart Tolle (b. 1948) is a German born spiritual teacher and writer. He changed his named from Ulrich Tolle because of his admiration for Meister Eckhart.* His best-known book, *The Power of Now* is a worldwide bestseller. As a young person, he suffered from long periods of depression.

KT Tunstall (b. 1975) is a Scottish singer songwriter. She has won the Ivor Novello song award. Her track 'Suddenly I See' was used by Hillary Clinton in her (failed) presidential campaign.

Mindfulness: A Practical Guide to Finding Peace in a Frantic World is an excellent book written by Prof Mark Williams* and Dr Danny Penman.

It forms an eight-week practical course (a sort of equivalent to the Alpha course for people starting out with Mindfulness). The book contains a CD with guided meditations for each of the 8 weeks.

Desmond Tutu (b. 1931) was a South African priest and theologian. He was the first black African to become a bishop and Archbishop in South Africa. He is perhaps best known for his work against apartheid and as the chair of the Truth and Reconciliation Commission which began in 1986. He is the winner of the Nobel Peace Prize and has written many books.

Ruby Wax (b. 1953) is a US born actress, comedian and mental health campaigner for which she has been awarded an OBE. She gained an MA in Mindfulness from the University of Oxford and has written two best-selling books about mindfulness *Sane New World* and *A Mindfulness Guide for the Frazzled*.

Mark Williams (b. 1952) Mark Williams is Emeritus Professor of Psychology at the University of Oxford. He co developed MBCT: Mindfulness Based Cognitive Therapy to help prevent relapse into the state of depression.

He is co-author with Danny Penman of *Mindfulness: A Practical Guide to Finding Peace in a Frantic World.** He is also an ordained priest.

CIRCLE
BOOKS

CHRISTIAN FAITH

Circle Books explores a wide range of disciplines within the field
of Christian faith and practice. It also draws on personal testimony
and new ways of finding and expressing God's presence in the
world today.

If you have enjoyed this book, why not tell other readers by
posting a review on your preferred book site. Recent bestsellers
from Circle Books are:

I Am With You (Paperback)
John Woolley

These words of divine encouragement were given to John Woolley
in his work as a hospital chaplain, and have since inspired and
uplifted tens of thousands, even changed their lives.
Paperback: 978-1-90381-699-8 ebook: 978-1-78099-485-7

God Calling
A. J. Russell

365 messages of encouragement channelled from Christ to two
anonymous "Listeners".
Hardcover: 978-1-905047-42-0 ebook: 978-1-78099-486-4

The Long Road to Heaven,
A Lent Course Based on the Film
Tim Heaton
This second Lent resource from the author of *The Naturalist and the Christ* explores Christian understandings of "salvation" in a five-part study based on the film *The Way*.
Paperback: 978-1-78279-274-1 ebook: 978-1-78279-273-4

Abide In My Love
More Divine Help for Today's Needs
John Woolley
The companion to *I Am With You*, *Abide In My Love* offers words of divine encouragement.
Paperback: 978-1-84694-276-1

From the Bottom of the Pond
The Forgotten Art of Experiencing God in the Depths of the Present Moment
Simon Small
From the Bottom of the Pond takes us into the depths of the present moment, to the only place where God can be found.
Paperback: 978-1-84694-066-8 ebook: 978-1-78099-207-5

God Is A Symbol Of Something True
Why You Don't Have to Choose Either a Literal Creator God or a Blind, Indifferent Universe
Jack Call
In this examination of modern spiritual dilemmas, Call offers the explanation that some of the most important elements of life are beyond our control: everything is fundamentally alright.
Paperback: 978-1-84694-244-0

The Scarlet Cord
Conversations With God's Chosen Women
Lindsay Hardin Freeman, Karen N. Canton
Voiceless wax figures no longer, twelve biblical women,
outspoken, independent, faithful, selfless risk-takers, come to life
in *The Scarlet Cord*.
Paperback: 978-1-84694-375-1

Will You Join in Our Crusade?
The Invitation of the Gospels Unlocked by the Inspiration of
Les Miserables
Steve Mann
Les Miserables' narrative is entwined with Bible study in this book
of 42 daily readings from the Gospels, perfect for Lent or anytime.
Paperback: 978-1-78279-384-7 ebook: 978-1-78279-383-0

A Quiet Mind
Uniting Body, Mind and Emotions in Christian Spirituality
Eva McIntyre
A practical guide to finding peace in the present moment that will
change your life, heal your wounds and bring you a quiet mind.
Paperback: 978-1-84694-507-6 ebook: 978-1-78099-005-7

Readers of ebooks can buy or view any of these bestsellers by
clicking on the live link in the title. Most titles are published in
paperback and as an ebook. Paperbacks are available in traditional
bookshops. Both print and ebook formats are available online.

Find more titles and sign up to our readers' newsletter at http://
www.johnhuntpublishing.com/christianity. Follow us on Facebook
at https://www.facebook.com/ChristianAlternative.